The 3 Questions

And the Answers that Could Save Your Life

Sean Forrest

ISBN: 978-1-4834-4378-2 (sc)
ISBN: 978-1-4834-4379-9 (e)

Lulu Publishing Services rev. date: 2/26/2016

Table of Contents

Introduction vii

Chapter 1   We're All Searching for Meaning 1

Chapter 2   Evil and Suffering—Where's God? 6

Chapter 3   Getting Out of the Boat 17

Chapter 4   The Three Questions 31

Chapter 5   Question 1: Does God Exist? 49

Chapter 6   Question 2: Then Who Is He? 71

Chapter 7   Oh, How He Loves Us 81

Chapter 8   The Resurrection: What It Is, What It Isn't,
             and Why It Matters 100

Chapter 9   The Bible: Is It Reliable? 121

Chapter 10   Question 3: What Is the Meaning of Life? 132

Resources for Life 139

Author's Note 141

Introduction

This book may scare you ... but that's okay. Because it's the kind of scared that helps you not be afraid anymore. That seems confusing, I know, but it isn't. It's the kind of scared that makes you open a closet door because you are convinced there is a monster inside—only to be relieved to discover that your fears were unwarranted. This book will scare you because it will ask you to really look at your deepest-held convictions about your faith in God—or your lack of faith in God—and make you ask yourself the question, "Do I really believe what I believe?" Think about it for a minute:

- Do you believe in God? If so, why? What evidence is there for God? If you don't believe in God, is that logical?
- Are you a Christian? If so, why? Does it matter what faith you are? If not, then why be a Christian?
- If I asked you to give me evidence that your faith in God, religion, or your belief system is true, could you? If not, there is a big problem.

Let's say you asked a doctor who was going to perform life-or-death surgery on you to show you his credentials and prove to you that he had the knowledge to do it. And let's say he told you he did not have any and that you should just trust him. Would you? I hope not! That's how absurd it is when a Christian tells someone that they have no evidence for their faith, but that they just feel strongly about it.

If you are going to believe something, you should know why you do. This book is designed to show you that belief in God and Christianity is reasonable. Our faith is NOT a blind faith. Trust me when I tell you that your faith will become even more alive and exciting when you see the reason behind it. It will no longer be simply a fantastic hope—a wish we make with our eyes closed and fingers crossed. Because God is not a mere creation in our own minds. Rather, He is the Great I Am, Who created us and gave us our minds so we can use reason to know Him. This awesome God Who created us spoke. We need to know what He said. For, once we know what God is saying to us, we can know why we are alive—and why our lives matter.

In these pages, you will discover the answers to the three most important questions a human being can ask. They are questions I have been asked over and over again, and they are questions that I had to first answer for myself so I knew I was following the Truth. This book outlines a dialogue I have with a girl named Emma. While Emma is not a real person, she represents a fusion of the many conversations and email communications I have had in my nineteen years of ministry.

Emma is an intelligent girl in her early twenties who has experienced the poor catechesis that often plagues the Church today. She has attended classes and done some reading on the faith, but has never truly learned or embraced the truth of the teaching. Together, we tackle the questions you've probably asked yourself … and hopefully guide you to some insightful answers.

This book is aimed at people between the ages of, oh, fourteen and 100—not an easy task! But, more importantly, it is for all those truly seeking answers. Some parts of the book will use my personal testimony to reach your heart, while other parts will be more cerebral, requiring you to really think deeply. This is not a quick twenty-page overview of Christianity, but an exploration of faith and reason. I realize that, in our culture today, fewer people are willing to devote the time and effort it takes to reach a deeper understanding of what we as Christians believe and why. But I know that these seekers are out there. You are one of them. You have proved it by picking up this book.

I am indebted to Dr. William Lane Craig, Bishop N.T. Wright, and Peter Kreeft for their brilliant works on the subjects in this book.

Sean Forrest

Chapter 1

We're All Searching for Meaning

Sean: So you're here because you want to know more about God?

Emma: Or if He even exists. I find myself at a real crossroads. I've studied religion before, but I must admit that I'm totally lost. It's like I'm both overwhelmed and underwhelmed with everything around me at the same time. I don't know. Life just seems stressful and pointless.

Someone told me I should talk to you because you helped him in his faith. But I don't want to believe in God just because someone else does or just because I find life meaningless. I want to believe in Him only if He's real.

Sean: I'm so sorry to hear that you've been struggling so much. And I agree that you should only believe in God if He's real. I'd love to talk this through—but I need you to promise that you'll hang with me today and not be afraid to really enter into this discussion.

Emma: I promise—but I am going to speak my mind and hold nothing back.

Sean: Same with me.

Emma: Okay, talk to me.

Sean: What I really need to do is answer three questions for you. Because until you get the answers to these three questions, nothing is going to change for you.

Emma: What? Just three questions answered? It can't be as easy as that.

Sean: No, not JUST three questions—but the most important three questions a human being can ask and find the answers to if he wants to really live and die well.

Emma: So tell me the answers to the three questions then!

Sean: It's not that simple, Emma. I really want you to go on a journey with me today so this all makes sense to you. And to do that, I need to start by sharing a little of my own story. It won't take too long, but I have to give you an idea of who I am and what I used to do.

Emma: Sounds good. Tell me your story.

Sean: Okay, so when I was little, my mother brought me to a church service that I'll never forget. It was almost two hours long, and I had to just sit there, not moving. The church was really small and packed with people, and it was a Protestant service where they really got into worship and praise. It seemed like it was 100 degrees in there, and all we had to cool things down were these ceiling fans that were blowing everybody's B.O. back down on top of us. The pastor was really boring and, forgive me … pathetic. He was a skinny, uptight dude who desperately wanted to be a cool Southern Baptist preacher who could get some reaction from the crowd.

Now picture it: I'm eleven years old, sitting with this big, fat tie on my neck and looking at this old bald guy right in front of me with sweat dripping down his back. I'm thinking, "You've got to be kidding me. I am not seeing God here, people!"

Emma: Wow, this sounds awful.

Sean: Oh, believe me, it was. So the pastor was up there repeating, "The Lord GAVE! The Lord GAVE!" And a woman would say, "Mmmm hmmmm," so he'd keep saying the word *gave* louder and louder, and the people would get louder and louder. After about twenty minutes of this, I was losing my mind. So just when I thought he was going to start another round of screaming "Gave!" I yelled, "COME ON!" really loud in front of the whole church—just at the moment that everyone got dead quiet. Everybody stopped and stared at me. My mom looked at me with eyes that said, "Be quiet, do you want to go to hell?" And I looked back, thinking, *I'm already there!* It was so uncomfortable—like something you would see in a movie.

Emma: I can totally see it!

Sean: I also remember that one of the other preachers there really scared us because he kept saying everyone in our church—except maybe ten people—was going to hell. So I told my mom I didn't want to go to heaven because I felt like God was scary. I pictured heaven being like that church service forever! Why would I want to do that forever when I couldn't even stand doing it for twenty minutes?

I had learned this distorted image of God, and I was afraid of God because I thought He was mean. Knowing better, my mom left that scary church, gave me a Bible for young teens, and told me to read it. She said, "I want you to read about Jesus, and you will see He is amazing and has a joyful heart."

So I did as she asked, and I came across this amazing story in the Bible that actually made me laugh out loud. I realized that God had a sense of humor, and it made Jesus much more real to me. Do you know the story where Peter walks on the water?

Emma: Sort of.

Sean: Well, that is the story that changed my life. Now, things may not have gone down *exactly* as I envisioned them when I read it, but sometimes Scripture can teach you and reach you one way—and then two days later it reveals something different, but equally amazing.

Anyway, I was reading the part where Jesus walked up to His disciples and said, "Hey guys see that boat? Get in it and head across the lake. I'll meet you on the other side later." They got in and took off, but soon the boat started getting "buffeted with waves." I pictured the disciples in the boat, with the wind sending waves over the bow. I could picture them getting nervous, holding on, and then all of a sudden start screaming.

Emma: Because of the waves?

Sean: No, the waves had them nervous, but they "became terrified crying out with fear" because they looked out onto the water and thought they saw a ghost. That's the word Scripture uses. Can you imagine these guys out at night getting pummeled with waves, wondering how things could get any worse, and a ghost shows up?!

But it would have been even worse. Because you know how when you're in a movie theater at a scary movie and all of a sudden one girl screams … and it ignites all the other girls to scream, too? That's the image I have of that boat. One guy screams and lights them all up. They think they see a ghost, but it's not a ghost after all. It's Jesus. And that's the part where I started cracking up.

Emma: What? Why?

Sean: Well, think about it. Jesus is God, which means He knows everything, so He *knows* they're going to be freaked out. He could have just showed up alongside the boat and said, "Hey guys, check it out!" And they would have thought, "Whoaaaa, most impressive!" But instead, He stood out on the water, while the apostles were screaming at the "ghost." I'm thinking He had to be laughing to Himself at that point, and I picture Him saying, "Ooooh ooooooh," like a ghost, because if I had that power, I'd totally mess with people. Of course, Scripture does not say that He did anything like that, but imagining it just cracked me up.

So then Jesus walked forward, shouting, "Guys relax, it's Me, it's the Lord." And for a minute they were probably relieved. "Oh, it's just Jesus!" But that would have quickly changed.

Emma: Why? Wouldn't they be excited to see Jesus? Well, maybe not to see Him walking on water ... now that I think about it ...

Sean: Exactly. They'd be terrified! If you and I hung out for three years and one day you're out in a boat in the middle of a lake miles from shore, and I just walk past you, you're not going to just say, "Hey, wear some sun block!"

Emma: Right.

Sean: So they were totally freaked out. Then Peter yelled something to Jesus that I'm sure he immediately regretted: "Jesus, if it's really You, command me and I'll walk out to You!" And you know right after he said it he thought, "Stupid, stupid, stupid! Man, just shut up for once!" But Jesus' response was brilliant: "Excellent. Come to Me."

So Peter stood up to walk out, took a step, and started walking on the water. With his eyes on Jesus, he was actually walking on water, being sustained by the gaze of Christ upon him. But then a wave hit him in the face, and he stopped looking at Jesus. In his doubt, he fell into the water.

Jesus picked him up by the hand and said, "Where's your faith?" You see, Peter was doing so well when he had his eyes on Jesus. And realizing *that* is why this story totally helped to change my life.

Think about it. When you're having a bad day, a bad week, a bad month or year, odds are you're not keeping your eyes on Jesus—but on yourself. That's where depression, anxiety, and fear all come from. We all know that we're going to fail ourselves. I fail myself all the time. So if I'm depending totally on myself and I try to walk on water, I'm going to sink. Of course I'm going to be nervous, depressed, and anxious a lot.

Emma: I would love to have someone in my own life who could keep me from drowning.

Sean: You do! But you need to trust that He's there.

Chapter 2

Evil and Suffering—Where's God?

Sean: Sometimes people who read that Bible story believe Jesus was mad at Peter because he didn't keep his eyes on Him. I don't buy that, you know why? Because Peter was the only one who had the courage to *get out of the boat.* Everybody else just sat there, and I think God is more pleased to see us at least try and fall than just sit there comfortably doing nothing.

To me, that is an analogy of many Christians today. Many people will go to church and hear what's being said, but they do nothing with it. They just keep it to themselves and stay in the boat because they're afraid to walk on water. Because getting out of the boat *is* scary and uncomfortable. The reality, though, is that if you really want to feel the comfort of Christ, you have to get uncomfortable.

So many people say things like, "But I don't feel the Lord." I say, "You'll feel the Lord when you're uncomfortable, when you're scared or frightened." The poor draw close to Jesus because Jesus was poor. People who suffer know God intimately. They draw close to Jesus because Jesus suffered. When we suffer, we can enter into a deep communion with God—especially if we unite that suffering with His.

Emma: Suffering and evil make it difficult for me to even *believe* in God, let alone unite my suffering with His. I don't really even know what that means!

Sean: I know, it sounds complicated. And it probably sounds crazy that good can come out of suffering. But it's true, so follow me here. I'm going to appeal first to your intellect and then to your heart to show how suffering can be beneficial—and how evil can even be a proof for God's existence.

Emma: How can evil and the suffering it causes be evidence for God? Do you seriously expect me to believe that?

Sean: Yes, I do. You are intelligent. If there is no God, there is no evil. If there is no God, then we can't even say Hitler was evil.

Emma: Of course I can!

Sean: You can say it, but you would be a hypocrite.

Emma: Why?

Sean: Think about it for a minute. If there is no God, then who determines what is evil?

Emma: People do.

Sean: Which people?

Emma: All people ... the majority of people determine what is right or wrong.

Sean: You must see how dangerous that line of thinking is, Emma. If all of society decided that slavery were okay, would that make it right?

Emma: Actually, no, it wouldn't. I see your point.

Sean: So, if we let society be the judge of what's right or wrong, we get horrible consequences, such as millions of people being declared non-human and in need of extermination.

Emma: The Nazis.

Sean: Communist Russia and China, too. Think about this. How would you tell Hitler he was "wrong" in what he was doing? Imagine you could have that conversation with him. Let me play Hitler, and you tell me why I am evil and wrong for killing six million Jews.

Emma: Okay, here we go. Hitler, murder is wrong.

Sean: Who says so?

Emma: I do!

Sean: I don't!

Emma: Society says it's wrong!

Sean: Not my society! Why are you pushing your values on me, acting as if they are superior to mine? Keep your values and your laws off of my body and mind. Who do you think you are?

Emma: Well, would you want someone to do it to *you?*

Sean: No. That's why I'm striking first to obtain power. Besides, you're an atheist, and you know we must live by Darwinian rules, survival of the fittest. We're doing society a favor by weeding out the weak so the strong can populate the earth and make a society of thoroughbreds. You don't seem to get upset when a fish eats another fish or when a fox catches a mouse. Why are you acting as if we're more special than the animals are?

Emma: Because I think it's wrong to kill!

Sean: You can think that, but it's just a thought. You don't mind animals being killed for food. Stop putting objective value on people. We're nothing but slime that has evolved! We have no soul or spirit inside us. We are a cosmic accident, and when we die we rot into the earth. There is no one keeping score. There is no judge. There is no heaven or hell.

Emma: Well maybe society has evolved, and we have learned that we do better when we don't kill each other!

Sean: If that were true, that just means evil is subjectively evil and not objectively evil, and maybe one day society may evolve back to find that murder is a good thing. I'm just helping society advance to this better state, to tolerate murder for the sake of the species.

Emma: This is freaking me out. I don't want to talk to Hitler anymore.

Sean: Good, but do you see what your argument comes down to? You said that perhaps killing each other is wrong because humans have evolved to see it that way. This means that torturing a small child isn't evil in and of itself, but only subjectively evil because we have evolved to think that way. Do you really believe that?

Emma: I don't know.

Sean: Of course you do. You know in your heart, mind, and soul that torturing a child is evil. You have a conscience that almost makes you sick to your stomach at the thought of it. God gave us this conscience. We did not have to "learn" that torturing a child is wrong. We know it to the core of our very being.

Emma: Yes ... I agree.

Sean: The problem for the atheist is that they can't live out atheism to its practical conclusions. In a world without God, there is no good and evil, no objective truth. An atheist can never say that something is objectively wrong or say the words, "You should not have..." We all know that there is a way things should be, and when it is not that way, we get upset. We all know that betraying a friend is a bad thing. People do it, but not because they think it's good.

Emma: I get it. If I punch an atheist, he can't say that it is wrong or evil. He can only say that he doesn't like getting punched. The minute he makes a truth statement, saying that punching is evil, he is either appealing to a higher authority or making himself the authority.

Sean: Exactly. And you can say that you think punching is good … and we have the Hitler conversation all over again.

Emma: So the fact that we know there is evil is evidence for God. If there were no God, then evil should not upset us because we are basically robots with no eternity awaiting us.

Sean: Just as pool balls on a table don't get upset when they smash apart, neither should we if there is no God. But we *do* get upset. We *do* feel pain and seek justice. Not only is there a God, but He is a God Who can bring about beauty through our suffering—especially when we enter into that suffering.

Emma: But why would you want to experience something like that? Why would you want to follow a religion where, instead of feeling joy, you have to suffer to be closest with God?

Sean: We experience God in joy and laughter, too, but remember that everyone will also suffer at some time in life. Christianity gives us *meaning* in that suffering. I can't explain why God allows it, but I do trust Him enough to know that He will bring about some greater good from it.

Emma: I don't know if I can buy that. Can you tell me when suffering ever helped anyone?

Sean: Yes, I can. First and foremost, Jesus' own suffering and death brought about the end of death. Heaven was opened, and we can be saved because of that suffering and death. Jesus does not ask us to walk where He has not. "Be not afraid, I go before you always."

Emma: I like that song.

Sean: Yes, it's a beautiful song—and it's taken from Scripture: "It is the Lord who goes before you; he will be with you and never fail you or forsake you. So do not fear or be dismayed" (Deuteronomy 31:8).

Emma: Okay, that's really powerful—if it's true.

Sean: I'm going to tell you about two situations in my own life where suffering really made a difference. The first is very personal and can be difficult to talk about. My wife Julie and I have lost twelve children to miscarriage.

Emma: Oh my gosh, I am so sorry! How come you're not mad at God?!

Sean: Because God doesn't do things to hurt us—He is the one Who saves. When Julie was losing our second child, it was brutal. She was so sick because her body was removing the child, but her heart was holding on. There was a battle of her will against nature, and that was making her very, very ill. She was dry heaving, she almost fainted, and she was in agony.

Emma: What did you do?

Sean: There comes a time in everyone's life when there is nothing you can do but give everything to God. I carried her to the bed and opened up the Bible and, while placing my hand upon her womb, I began to read Psalms to her from Scripture and asked God to help ease the pain of my wife. I asked Him to use this suffering of ours to help protect all babies, especially the unborn. I also asked God to give me her suffering if He would. We both suffered because we were parents already. People don't become parents just when the baby is born; when she conceived, there was a soul there. We already loved this child so much. In fact, we have a marker with all the names of our children who died too soon.

Emma: Did her pain go away when you prayed?

Sean: You know, it did in a way. While she was still in agony, I looked over at her eyes while praying over her, and she was watching me. She put her hand on mine and said, "In my darkest hour, you are leading me to

Jesus. I trust you with everything." In that moment, we both fell more deeply in love with each other than ever before. In that moment, we also experienced the grace of God binding us together ever more deeply. We had the strong realization that God would be taking care of that child and all of our children.

Emma: Okay, I can't believe it, but you actually just showed me how suffering can be beautiful. I can't stop crying.

Sean: I'm sorry to upset you.

Emma: No, this is actually a good cry. For once, I'm crying about something beautiful instead of painful.

Sean: Can you see now how the loss of our child is even helping you, as well?

Emma: Yes. I actually do.

Sean: Shortly, I'm going to show you another time when God used suffering in my life in a profound way. So profound that without it I would not even be here speaking to you.

Emma: But I don't want to suffer.

Sean: It's not about wanting to suffer, but about trusting that if that's what God is asking of us, He's using it for good. There's something called redemptive suffering, where God uses the suffering offered up by people as a way to convert hearts, or bring about the end of poverty, or bring about conversion. So if I have the flu, I'm going to offer that suffering up and pray something like this, "Father in heaven, I offer my suffering for the conversion of my uncle, myself, and the whole world."

Evil never wins because if our suffering can be used to bring about love and conversion, then even in our agony we can help to bring people to God. Also, it's often when we're in our darkest times that we draw close to God and really start to rely on Him.

But I also don't want you to think that faith is only about suffering. It's definitely not! It's about love, joy, and hope. I'm just saying that I know God did not just put us on this earth so we could consume and die. Life is an adventure. Trust me when I tell you, when you get out of the boat and walk with Christ, it's then that your life will get exciting!

Emma: That actually makes sense.

Sean: When you're constantly feeling content and getting everything you need and more, there tends to be a spirit of complacency. Some who live like this often forget to give thanks. I wonder how many people in America say grace before each meal. Think about this: Every 3.6 seconds, someone starves to death. Twenty thousand people starved to death today. 1.6 million children starve to death every year. There is more than enough food to feed everyone in the world easily. So, is it God's fault that there are starving people?

Emma: No, I guess not …

Sean: That's right. Not to be judgmental, but I don't understand how a human being who is well-off can go to bed at night and sleep easily, knowing they have done nothing whatsoever to help ease the hunger of a starving person either through money, work, or prayer. The thought that a little girl just died from hunger and is being eaten by rats right now can keep me up at night, you know?

Emma: I guess I've never really spent much time thinking about it. I think we get so busy that it slips our minds.

Sean: That's my point. Many people seem to get so busy that they forget about what matters. I'm not saying wealth is bad. Many generous people have helped financially to build an orphanage and mission that my organization runs in Haiti. I am talking about those who have truly forgotten what Scripture tells us. James 1:27 says: "Religion that is pure and undefiled before God the Father is this: to care for orphans and widows in their distress, and to keep oneself unstained by the world."

Emma: So being a Christian is about helping the poor.

Sean: That's only part of it. Many people have this confused. Being a Christian is not just about doing good deeds. That is actually a very dangerous path. We start to think we are holy because we help the poor and therefore deserve to go to heaven and honor God with our presence. Concepts like Liberation Theology and social justice theology are dangerous and wrong. They turn Jesus' message of love, forgiveness, sin, repentance, and redemption into a violent revolution concerned only about bringing equal pay to the world.

First and foremost, we must recognize that we have all fallen short of the kingdom of heaven. We need a Savior to … well … save us! My blood is not holy enough to save myself from the sins of our first parents, the sins of the world, and the sins I have committed. Only Jesus' blood can do that.

Emma: Did Jesus die only for Christians?

Sean: No! Check this out. It's a snippet from the Catholic Answers (*Catholic.com*) website that I think will help you: "Jesus died for the redemption of all mankind. The apostle Paul says, 'For to this end we toil and strive, because we have our hope set on the living God, who is the Savior of all men, especially of those who believe' (1 Timothy 4:10). God desires the salvation of all men (cf. 1 Timothy 2:3-4), thus He died to redeem mankind and offer salvation to all. His death redeemed mankind collectively, so we can say that even non-Christians are redeemed. Because each person has free will, he can choose to reject the salvation offered him as a gift. So, while all are redeemed, it is possible that not all will be saved. Christ's death is sufficient for the salvation of all, but it is efficient for the salvation of those who choose to accept that gift." Does that make sense?

Emma: So God loves us all, regardless of religion. He died for us all then, right?

Sean: Exactly! But if we forget that we need to get right with God and confess our sins, keep the commandments, and live the beatitudes, we start to forget why Jesus came in the first place and turn Him into a zealous hippie. Jesus suffered and died for all of our sins.

Emma: His suffering, you are saying, saved the world.

Sean: Yes, and He's asking us to turn to Him in our own suffering. To keep our eyes on Him—like Peter on the water—and trust that He is there for us.

Emma: I guess when you take your eyes off of yourself, that's when you actually do get to see Jesus. So it makes sense that it would be in our darkest hours that we see Jesus because it's then that we start looking out for help—and our eyes can find Him. If we're suffering with our eyes on Christ, it's possible for something good to come out of it.

Sean: You are getting it! So without God, suffering *is* meaningless. It's nothing. Without God, suffering is not "bad" or "evil"—it's just part of a cruel, random universe. Only with God can we find meaning in it.

Emma: Does God reveal to us the meaning of life, then? Because I just really need to *know*. Why am I alive? Is there hope? I'm sick of being afraid!

Sean: I completely understand. I totally get your fear, but know this: When we seek God, He doesn't just magically take away our fears. He gives us the courage to face them because we do not face them alone. Of course God did and does perform miracles, but following Jesus isn't like having a genie in a lamp who pops up and then "Poof!" your problems go away. He is so much greater than that. He is real. He is God. And He is crazy about you.

Emma: I so want to believe that, but I need to be sure.

Sean: Let's keep going then. I'm impressed that you are using your mind like this. Don't fall for propaganda. Fall for truth.

Emma: I'm trying to have an open mind.

Sean: Be careful, though. Let me quote the author G.K. Chesterton: "Do not be so open-minded that your brains fall out." I think this quote of his will also serve us well: "Merely having an open mind is nothing. The object of opening the mind, as of opening the mouth, is to shut it again on something solid."

When I was doing my own searching like you are, I found that "something solid," and it helped me to get out of the boat for the very first time.

Chapter 3

Getting Out of the Boat

Sean: That story about Peter getting out of the boat has a lot to do with my journey. My own first "getting out of the boat" moment goes back many years to when, by the world's standards, I had the "perfect life."

For many years, I was a bar musician/entertainer, and I started making a lot of money doing that. I had a nice condo, with four private beaches, a sail boat, a fishing boat, nice cars, and a beautiful wife. We'd go to the islands often. I was making really good money playing out. Most everybody liked me, and the bar owners thought I was great because I could solicit alcohol like nobody's business. I had sponsorships from certain companies that would actually pay me to drink their alcohol in public.

I was playing at this one area up in Killington, Vermont, and everybody liked me because I was this great party guru. But in my heart, I was having a dilemma. None of my friends knew it, but when I was in junior high I wanted to be a pastor.

Emma: What? Really?

Sean: Yeah, I know. Nobody would have ever guessed it, but I was really thinking God was calling me to be a minister. But I learned to play the guitar—and girls like that. And then I started making money in bars, so I started thinking, "Well, I'll be a pastor some other day. Right now I'm gonna party and do whatever I want and get paid to do it." I also had a lot of scars from childhood that ran deep, and instead of letting Jesus heal me, I went off the deep end a bit in rebellion. I truly lost my way.

Emma: I see that happen to a lot of people.

Sean: So there I was playing up at this ski resort and making a lot of money. Halfway through the show, I would always do a toast and take a shot of alcohol. I would hold it up, everyone would gather, and I would make up a limerick—and it was always inappropriate. The people would cheer, and I'd get a bonus from the alcohol sponsors, who paid me to encourage people to drink their brand. I worked six hours a week, and I was making more than my college-educated friends. I had it all.

Emma: That sounds great!

Sean: Yeah, I know. Then one day, right after I sang Jimmy Buffet's "Margaritaville," a very drunk man came up to me and said, "Will you play Jimmy Buffet's 'Margaritaville'?" I said, "Sir, you just danced to it." He was so drunk, he had absolutely no idea what was going on. It really hit me.

I started looking around, thinking, "Man, I'm not judging these people, but I'm not sure this is what I'm supposed to be doing with my life." But I was surrounded by people who kept encouraging my behavior, and it made it difficult to stop. I don't blame them. Hey, I was an adult. But it's difficult to listen to your conscience when your ego is being fed and overflowing to cover the wounds of childhood. No one ever said a negative thing to me until "he" showed up.

Emma: He? Who is "he"?

Sean: Sorry, I just wanted to add emphasis to this brief, but dramatic, encounter. He was a priest from the surrounding area.

Emma: Really? What did he want?

Sean: To ruin me.

Emma: What?! Was he a jerk or something?

Sean: No, he was actually a man of courage and honor. I was on stage surrounded by fans, and he walked over to me and asked me to lean down so he could speak to me. I remember it so clearly. I asked him what he wanted, and he said, "You should take off your cross. I can't judge your soul, but if I were a betting man I would be pretty safe in thinking that if you died today you would go straight to hell. If you remove the cross, at least you won't be scandalizing these people, as well."

Emma: No way! What a jerk!

Sean: That's all he said, and then he walked out. I was furious. How dare he say that to me? I make people happy! I am the entertainer! I am a good person! I am … I am … full of crap.

Emma: What?

Sean: Yes, Emma. Because he nailed it on the head. I had people who were coming to my shows instead of going to Mass. I had watched people become alcoholics, and instead of helping them, I went right along collecting money from their drink sales—all while wearing a decorative cross around my neck. I knew what I was doing was wrong, but I justified it. That priest was amazing to call me out on it.

Emma: You think he was amazing?

Sean: Let me share a Bible verse with you, Proverbs 28:23: "Whoever rebukes another wins more favor than one who flatters with the tongue." That priest sent a spiritual shockwave through me. It started to awaken the man of faith I had buried. Sometimes the patient is near death and needs the paddles. This priest supplied that for me.

Emma: So did you leave the bar scene?

Sean: Well … not exactly. It took a little longer than that. Remember, my whole livelihood was funded by this career. I had no college degree, so what else could I do? As you can see, my trust level in God was a bit shallow at the time. But my questioning of what I was doing with my life—and the challenge of that priest—were the beginning of the end of that period of my life.

Emma: This is when you got out of the boat.

Sean: It was the start. Though I was still at the bars doing shows, one day I had this very intense moment. I had started talking to God, reading, and praying. Almost no one knew any of this. I had told one other fellow musician and one good friend about my new desire to seek God and how I was uncomfortable playing in bars. When I told my friend, he said, "Do you like your condo on the beach?" I told him, "Of course." He replied, "Then shut up and keep playing at the bar." But I was really worrying because New Year's Eve was coming up, and that's when I would renew my contract with the liquor companies. It was also the night of the big toast in front of almost 1,500 people.

Emma: The toast with the limerick that you would do in front of the crowd?

Sean: Yes. So finally New Year's Eve came, and I found myself at a crossroads moment. I still wasn't sure what I was going to do that night when the time for the toast arrived. To make things more complicated, earlier that afternoon something strange had happened. I was sitting in my condo right down the road from the bar, when there was a knock on my door. When I opened it, these three local musicians were standing there. I hardly knew them, but they said, "Hey, look, we know you're looking for God."

Emma: It had leaked out like that?

Sean: It was a small town, and rumors spread quickly. Everyone kind of knew everything about everyone. So they said, "Look we want to encourage you to do it." And I said, "Okay, thanks, but I feel really uncomfortable. I don't like talking about God that much." As I was escorting them out of the condo, one of them handed me a rosary. They were Catholics, and I didn't know much about Catholics then. I pretty much thought they were all a bunch of crazy people, so I encouraged them to go away, and I shut the door.

So it was New Year's Eve, and I was having these internal struggles. There were all these shots lined up on the stage, ready for the toast. The alcohol representatives were there, as well. Everyone was waiting for me to do my big toast, and I was having this big battle rage inside me: *Do I want to do this? Can I really do this?* Talk about peer pressure! My whole livelihood, the money I was making, the condos … everything was coming from those shows. I was liked. I drank for free. I ate for free. I became a celebrity. I knew lots of great people. That place helped to cover my wounds.

Emma: So what happened?

Sean: I got up on stage thinking, *Okay, maybe I'll just do the toast.* I started to cave. But this is a really cool part of the story. In the bar was a balcony, and under the balcony were a bunch of tables and chairs. I looked over, and at a table underneath the balcony were those three Catholic guys … praying a Rosary for me in the bar.

Emma: I have the chills now.

Sean: It was crazy. I didn't even know what a rosary was. I didn't know what it did. It looked like a weapon. Well, turns out, it is—a weapon against the devil. Now people above them started pouring beer on their heads from the balcony because those guys were praying. Those three men did not run up there to fight them, and they wouldn't leave. They knew there was a spiritual battle going on for me that nobody else knew was going on. Even to this day, few people know this went down.

But this is the thought that went through my head: *I don't know who these three guys are, but they love me more than anybody in this bar. I don't know anyone else who'd let someone dump a beer on his head for praying for me.*

And I didn't do the toast.

Emma: You didn't do it?!

Sean: I didn't do it. I grabbed my guitar, and I said, "Hey, I've got something special for you all tonight. I wrote a song instead!" And they shouted, "Is it about alcohol?!" And I said, "Not exactly." No one knew I had written a song about Peter walking on the water.

Emma: No way! You played it?

Sean: I played it that night for everybody. The chorus goes, "It's so easy. Just keep your eyes on Me. It's so easy. Just let your faith flow free ..." Now the funny thing is that I taught them the entire chorus, but they didn't really know what it was about. So they just started singing, thinking eventually it would be about alcohol. There were 1,500 people holding beers and shots singing, "It's so easy ..." I just picture God looking down from heaven saying, "Hey, that's nice ... er umm ... okay ... close enough ... hmmm ... wow ..."

Emma: That is crazy!

Sean: Speaking in front of people is difficult enough, but publicly singing a song that you wrote from your heart is terrifying, especially when it's one you wrote about God and you live in the secular world that I did. THAT was the moment when I got out of the boat.

Emma: Like Peter.

Sean: Yes. It was the moment I decided I really wanted to find and follow God and see if it all was real. It wasn't necessarily about becoming a Catholic—that came later—but I was on a mission.

Emma: What happened when you finished the song?

Sean: The entire place went nuts cheering! They were cheering and screaming, and people started praying and worshipping God, and they lifted me up in the air ... and if that were true it'd be the coolest story EVER.

Emma: Hey, you actually had me believing that!

Sean: Sorry, but no. I received a sympathetic clap from a few people, but many were looking at me thinking, "What the heck just happened to Sean?" And it was weird. It got really weird.

Emma: I feel awkward just hearing about it. Must have been a really bad moment.

Sean: Oh, yeah. Within three months, I was completely out of work at my other gigs back in Connecticut. No one would come see the shows anymore.

Emma: Wow, your whole life changed overnight.

Sean: Yes, but it was okay. And I did know there was someone there who supported me at that Killington bar. There was a manager with the nickname "Tuna." I think he was an atheist, but I'm not sure. He'd never speak of spiritual things, and he prided himself on managing this huge money-making machine.

Yet, after almost every show, he would call me into his office and say, "You should stop partying on stage. You're a good musician. You can do better things, you know?" But partying had become such a part of our show, and that's how we made the money.

Emma: If you didn't drink, would people go?

Sean: The more I drank, the more the crowd drank. The more the crowd drank, the more money the bar made. The more money the bar made, the more I got paid. So I got paid to drink.

But Tuna was constantly telling me, "To hell with the crowd, take care of yourself." I share this with anybody who ever had a friend die who was not a believer. Jesus said, "When I was in prison, you visited me." You see, Tuna as an atheist was a better friend to me than every baptized friend I had in that bar. He, that priest, and the guys praying the Rosary for me

23

were practically the only ones to speak truth into my life. I was in a prison, and Tuna saw that. He visited me there, opening the door for a way out.

I'm always thankful for this man who cared more about me than liquor sales. In helping me, he was really reaching out to the lost. When we reach out to the lost, we have the chance to encounter Christ in the process. And when we encounter Christ, there is always hope.

Emma: That's a very comforting thought.

Sean: We should always hope in Christ. Nothing is impossible for Him. The best thing that ever happened to me was singing that song on stage. When I put out my first CD of Christian music, I put a line in there that said, "When I was drinking and partying to excess, everyone used to cheer for me. When I became a Christian and a devoted husband, everyone started saying, 'I'm worried about Sean. I think he has a problem.'" How ironic.

Emma: So what did your wife think?

Sean: The whole thing was pretty amazing, actually. In many relationships, when one spouse finds faith in God and starts going to church, it can upset the other spouse, who gets jealous or uncomfortable. There can be a really tough "breaking-in period" during that time, especially if it is the wife who finds faith first. Guys are usually like, "Oh no ... Please not that! ... There is no way I'm missing football on Sundays! ... Do we have to say grace now? ... Who is this woman?"

Emma: You are totally cracking me up!

Sean: Funny, but sad.

Emma: So how *did* your wife take it?

Sean: I'm afraid that the beauty of this moment will not translate well, but here goes. My wife, Julie, had been going to Mass all along, though she wasn't really sure why. That was about the extent of her faith. She had become like many cradle Catholics who are mostly Catholic in name only. And I was one of those people who thought I was a good guy, so God would let me into heaven.

Well, driving home one day, I was at a 7-11 and there was a CD on the counter with two songs on it. They were Christian songs. I listened to them on my drive home, and they melted my heart. They were titled, "Follow the Fisher of Men" and "Seize the Day." Perfect songs for that time in my life, and God planted them exactly where they needed to be.

I brought the CD into our condo, and I lay on the floor. I asked Julie to lie by my side, and I told her I wanted her to hear the songs. When they finished, I told her that I wanted to start following God and praying. The moment is difficult to explain. It was a Holy Spirit moment, and we were completely connected. It is almost like our marriage really took the life it was designed to take, right then and there on the floor, lying side by side and holding hands. We had finally chosen to make room for God in our marriage. Words fail me here. I'm sorry.

Emma: No, I get it. Wow.

Sean: We sat there for about an hour, listening to those two songs over and over again. I can't tell you what a blessing it was for both of us to have come into faith at the same time. It was as if my "Yes" to God opened the floodgates for Julie, too. My heart goes out to anyone who loves God but has a spouse who does not want to enter into that together. It is so difficult. I always tell them to pray and be patient—and wait upon the Lord. You will win them over with kindness and prayer, but never if you force it.

Emma: So beautiful. And you were done with the bar business.

Sean: Sorry, but not just yet. Yes, I stopped partying at the bars and lost a lot of work, but I still had Killington, and I needed to make a living. God had to really get my attention to convince me to leave my livelihood completely. I made a huge mistake.

Emma: What?

Sean: God wanted to bring me on a journey, but I still wanted to stay comfortable. I had gotten out of the boat by letting people know I believed in God, but did not realize the plans God really had for me. He wanted me out of the boat and walking through tidal waves! So, God kept tugging at my heart to go deeper, and when summer came … it happened.

Emma: Oh no, whenever you talk like that something crazy is about to happen.

Sean: You are getting to know me pretty well!

I was looking out at my sail boat from my condo window thinking, "Man, I have just about everything I need, everything I want," when all of a sudden my chest started feeling really tight and pain was shooting down my arm. I thought I was having a heart attack and that I was going to die. I can't explain the fear to you unless you have ever experienced that feeling of "I'm going to die. I'm going to die now!"

Two thoughts went through my head. My first thought was that my wife was going to find me dead on the floor—and though she was the most amazing woman in the world, she really needed a man of God to help inspire her to live her faith more deeply, and I had failed to be that man. My second thought was that I wasn't ready to face God. I had been given gifts, and I used them all to help build my career, make money, and help keep people where they were, not elevate them. I justified everybody's partying by convincing myself that they needed to let off steam instead of seeing that many of them were really broken deep inside. They used my happy hour show as a church service to numb themselves for a few hours. No real healing was happening.

Now God is merciful, but I knew there was so much more I could have done with my life to help others and serve God—and I had failed to do that. I was once asked, "If you were before a judge and on the stand for claiming to be a Christian, would there be enough evidence to convict you of being a Christian?" Honestly, the answer for me at that moment was "No."

So I was clutching my chest thinking, *If I die now, I will stand before a God who is going to hold out His hands with holes in them and ask, "Did you really love me? Did you really seek to know me? Did you really keep my commandments? Did you care for my lost, my lonely, and my poor?"* And all I had to say was, "No, I didn't." In John 14:15, Jesus says, "If you love me, keep my commandments." Wearing a cross is not enough.

Emma: If I'm really honest with myself, I'm afraid I would have to give the same answer. So you had a heart attack?

Sean: No, I didn't have a heart attack. I had a panic attack. A full-scale, ten-out-of-ten on the panic scale anxiety attack. I had never heard of anything like that in my life. There's a lot more to this part of the story, such as a long-lasting illness, but let's just say God was getting my attention.

Emma: Suffering can lead you to God, right?

Sean: Yes it can—and it did.

Emma: Why the panic attacks?

Sean: I had buried old wounds and fears—but they weren't dead. You see, God is a relationship. He loves us and desires us to love Him back, totally and completely. In my bar days, I was surrounded by people who told me what I wanted to hear, but they were just giving me more manure to throw on the compost pile that covered the demons I had buried. Jesus doesn't play like that. He looks at us and says, "Do you really want to love me? If so, we need to dig up those things you buried and heal your heart." That's why many people run from Jesus. He doesn't tell you what you want to hear, but tells you what you *need* to hear because He loves you.

Emma: That sounds really scary.

Sean: At first it does seem scary, but we do not walk alone. He goes with us. You see, therapy is good, and people should take advantage of it if they can find a good therapist, but therapy can't fully heal you or save you. Only

Jesus can do that. You need to take what you discover in therapy and bring it before the Lord.

You may unlock and divulge that you were abused and have hatred towards some person. The therapist can help you to find coping techniques for that, but you need more than that. You need to be healed. Jesus will comfort you and give you the grace to forgive the person, and once you can honestly do that, then you are truly free. Freedom does not just come from recognizing our wounds. It comes from letting God heal them and give us the grace to love and forgive.

Emma: A lot of people have hurt me. When I think about it, I guess I hide my rage with sarcasm and music.

Sean: I'm glad you trust me enough to share that. I'm so sorry you've been hurt. Do you see, though, that the sarcasm and music are the dirt you're using to bury the demon?

Emma: Yeah, I see what you mean.

Sean: Now for me, some people would say that the panic attacks were cruel things for me to go through. I tell them they couldn't be more wrong. I wouldn't trade them for anything. Sure, in the midst of suffering, I couldn't see God's plan, but now that I can see the whole picture, I'm so thankful for that suffering.

Emma: But how can you say that? I have panic attacks and struggle with anxiety, too. They're awful—and I'm feeling a bit anxious right now.

Sean: Should we stop?

Emma: No, I guess I just don't understand how they are a blessing.

Sean: Let's see if this example helps you. Imagine you have a wound on your arm. It constantly bothers you, so you frequently go to see a person who puts ointment on it. That relieves the pain for a little while, but you know deep down that tomorrow the pain is coming back. The pain is letting you know that there is a wound that needs to be healed, but you keep going to someone who only helps the symptoms. Finally you go to a surgeon, and he opens up that wound. It hurts like crazy, but he cleans it out and stitches you up—and it is finally healed.

Jesus is the Divine Physician. He does not put Band-Aids on old wounds. He opens them up and heals them. Surgery sounds scarier than a Band-Aid, but after the surgery you are so thankful to finally be healed. In life, Band-Aids take many forms: alcohol, sex, drugs, work, pornography, etc. People who use these Band-Aids are not "bad" people. They are just wounded and want to alleviate the pain for a short spell until the next wave of pain, fear, loneliness, depression, or anxiety comes over them. But what they need is Jesus. He heals. He restores. He makes all things new. I love this quote from St. Augustine: "Our hearts are restless, Lord, until they rest in thee."

Emma: That is a good quote. I know that I have tried numbing myself with alcohol, drugs, sex, music, and relationships. And I'm still struggling to find meaning in my life and still having panic attacks. So there has to be something else, or I'm finished.

Sean: There is something else. Hang in there. We still have a journey to take here, but I think it will be worth your while to stay.

My own panic attacks were letting me know that it was time for surgery. No more Band-Aids. It was time for the wounds to be unburied so I could finally be freed of them. I would rather enter into my wounds with Jesus and be healed than live in fear, numbing myself every four hours.

Emma: Do you really think Jesus can help me, too?

Sean: Yes, He can help you, and He has been longing for you to let Him.

Emma: Okay, I think I want you to continue. Tell me more about your panic attacks.

Sean: Well, that first panic attack just about killed me. It was such an eye opener. I realized that, though I thought I had everything in the world, I still wasn't really happy. I didn't have peace. Most of the people who knew me didn't know this, but I was struggling brutally with an interior battle between that little boy who wanted to be a pastor and the wounded ego that said defensively, "You know what, I like making money, having people notice me, and having fun. This lifestyle lets the demons stayed buried!" But my ability to justify evil started destroying me inside. So I had this major panic attack and then a flurry of smaller ones, and I was in a constant state of anxiety. It was that anxiety that forced me to pray and forced me to think.

I eventually realized that my faith in God had been mostly emotional, and my reason was contradicting it. If God was going to use me, I needed to be much more solid in my faith. I had to be sure that it was reasonable to believe in God. Then it came to me. In order for me to follow God with all my heart, mind, soul, and strength, I needed the answers to three key questions.

I have been sharing these questions—and the answers to them—with people for the last nineteen years of my life. And now I want to share them with you.

Chapter 4

The Three Questions

Emma: Wow. Okay, so we are finally at the three questions!

Sean: I truly believe that without these three questions being answered, we're going to keep seeing a rise in suicide, depression, anxiety, divorce, abortion, and alcoholism. If priests, CCD teachers, directors of religious education, and youth ministers can't answer these questions, then we are in trouble. But it is the parents who really need to be able to answer these questions. If parents can't answer these questions, they will be lost—and their children will be even more lost. They will be blindsided by the world.

Emma: I can't stand when parents make their kids go to church but don't go themselves. My mom did that to me. If parents aren't going to church, then why are the kids expected to go?

Sean: Good question! And what's worse is the divide-and-conquer approach. If mom goes to church and drags the kids, but dad doesn't, mom is always the bad guy. The statistics I've seen show that if the mother goes to church with her children but the father doesn't go, only 17% of the kids will continue to go to church when they go off to college. If dad goes to church with the kids and mom doesn't go, 87% will continue.

Emma: Wow, that shows how important the father is in all of this. And it clarifies a lot in my own family situation. My father bailed on us.

Sean: Sorry to hear that, Emma.

Emma: Yeah, we just did our best to hold it all together. Just keep going, though. For some reason, I'm nervous to hear what the three questions are.

Sean: Don't be nervous. Be excited because they are life-changing questions. They are the questions I pray the Church will focus on, especially now.

So, the FIRST QUESTION is this: Does God really exist? And, if He's really there, how do I know? What proof is there? Emma, my brain is not a sucker's brain.

Emma: Excuse me?

Sean: My brain needs evidence to believe in things. My grandparents just had the gift of faith. I didn't have that.

Emma: But how do you know beyond faith?

Sean: Great question. We use reason. Faith is not about believing in the unreasonable. Faith is putting trust in something that seems reasonable. Let me give you an example.

If you were driving down the road on the coast of Maine for three hours, and the road went around a bend and you couldn't see it anymore, you wouldn't just stop driving, thinking, *Whoa ... I'd better stop driving because the road may not be there around the bend!* No, you would keep driving because the evidence is that for the past three hours the road has been there, and odds are it will be there as you come around the bend. The same goes for faith in God. I can't see around the "bend" of the invisible God, but the evidence is that He will be there when I come around the corner. The evidence leads us to say that it is logical to believe in God.

Emma: So, there is evidence for God's existence?

Sean: Yes there is, Emma. *Good* evidence.

Emma: You can actually prove that God exists?

Sean: No, what I am saying is that there is great evidence for His existence that allows me to reasonably put my faith in Him.

Emma: Okay, I get that.

Sean: My brain needs to see the math. I need to know 2+2=4. I want to write it out. I want to see it and think, "That makes sense, that's logical." I don't want to believe in illogical things. Some people are just given the gift of faith. Not me. I could go to my grandmother and say, "How do you know God exists?" And she'd say, "I can feel Him in my heart." I'd be thinking, *I can feel pizza in my stomach and it's warm and it makes me smile, but that doesn't mean I am going to worship it.*

You know, lots of people believe in strange things because they make them feel comforted. But how can that comfort you if it's not real? I actually had a friend who told me that when he dies, he believes he'll become a pixie.

Emma: A pixie? Are you kidding? Did that make him feel good?

Sean: It did.

Emma: Was it just to make a joke about death?

Sean: No, he really believed that when he died, heaven would be whatever he wanted it to be, and he wanted to be a pixie. There are a lot of movies that portray that false vision of heaven as being your own creation, and unfortunately people will believe just about anything if a favorite movie star says it.

Emma: So what did you say to him?

Sean: I said, "So heaven is whatever you want it to be?" And he said, "Yes, if you believe it sincerely enough, that means it's true. It's your truth." So I said, "If I believe something sincerely enough, that makes it true?" When he said, "Yes," I said, "I sincerely believe I'm a pony right now." He looked at me, and I said, "Dude, how come I didn't become a pony? I sincerely believed it." He said, "Well it only works for when you die."

I looked at him again and said, "Let me get this straight. If I believe sincerely enough in something, then it's true, right?" And he once again said, "Yes!" So I said, "If you jump out of a plane without a parachute, but you sincerely believe you have one, you will die!" I can envision the man jumping and pulling the rip cord, shouting, "I sincerely believe!" No, you're sincerely wrong, you idiot, and now you're sincerely dead.

Sincerity doesn't mean something is true. Then I said, "What if someone sincerely believes that when they die their heaven is going to be sincerely killing you every day." And he said, "Hey! That's brutal!" I replied, "Well, too bad. It's my truth."

I mean, if everybody's truth is true, that means *nobody's* truth is true. We're all full of BS, and we know it.

Emma: But how do you know your truth is true? Because there are other people who really do believe that their truth is true. When we get down to it, don't most people believe in the religion of their culture and where they were raised? For example, Americans will most likely be Jews or Christians, and people from India will usually be Hindus. When you look at it like that, faith isn't about objective truth, but custom.

Sean: While it is true that many people hold onto the faith or philosophy they inherited, that does not make their faith or philosophy true. Let me quote the Catholic apologist Trent Horn here: "Just because someone is born in a place where they fail to discover the right answer about life's important questions does not mean there are no right answers. This goes for any truth claim."

Think about it. If you lived in the eighteenth century, you most likely would have supported the enslavement of Native Africans. You don't think that would have been right, do you?

Emma: Absolutely not.

Sean: And if you were raised under the thumb of Nazi Germany during the terror of Hitler, you most likely would have supported the killing of Jews. I know you would see that as wrong.

Emma: I totally see your point, but how do you know your faith is true?

Sean: Glad you asked. That's why we are here talking today. St. John Paul II wrote a great encyclical that everyone should read called *Fides et Ratio*, which means "Faith and Reason." Faith is a gift from God, but God has also given us the gift of our intellect. We must use both faith and reason together to make sure what we believe is reasonable and good. Otherwise, you start believing really weird things like: The trees are God, you are God, and the chair is God—or that we don't even exist. Remember, sincerity doesn't mean truth. I—and all of us—must go on this intellectual journey, along with prayer, to figure out the answers to these questions.

Let me give an example. A friend of mine died, and I was freaked out. His father came up to me and said, "Listen Sean, I'm giving Jimmy's eulogy. I can see that you and the rest of the boys are shaken up, but I'm going to make you all feel better when I tell you about where Jimmy is now." I was excited because I wanted to know. I wanted to know what was true. I wanted to know if Jimmy's dad was going to take away my fear of death.

He got up to the pulpit and said, "My Jimmy loved the gray wolves of America." And I just looked at him. My eyes got wide, and I was thinking, *What did he just say?* And he said it again, "My Jimmy loved the gray wolves." And he did. Jimmy had posters of gray wolves all over his walls, but I started thinking, *Where is he going with this?* He continued, "Therefore, I know my Jimmy is now a gray wolf. When you look out and see a pack of gray wolves, you'll see the pack leader, and you'll know that's my Jimmy leading the way." I meant no disrespect, but when we left, I told my friends that Jimmy's dad was full of BS. They told me to stop it, but I said, "I'm serious, man, you go pet Jimmy and he'll eat you!" You know what I'm saying?

Emma: Jimmy's dad sounded like your buddy and the pixie thing all over again.

Sean: Exactly! Jimmy's dad had the right to say that, but I was left wondering, *How could he know that was true? How can you believe that reasonably?* Come on, man. I'm not trying to make fun of anybody or any religion, but do we want to believe in what is true or delude and numb ourselves with fantasy? Believing that when you die you get to choose your heaven is a blind leap of illogical faith, and that is too big a gamble for me! Faith is something that should have reason behind it. I'm not interested in blind faith because to me that is just fantasy. At that point, you may as well worship Mickey Mouse.

If Jimmy's dad could reasonably show me how evidence drew him to the conclusion that his son is now the leader of a gray wolf pack, then he would have my interest. Unfortunately, there is no evidence whatsoever that Jimmy is now a wild animal. Most likely, Jimmy's father did not know how to cope with the loss of his son and was grasping at straws.

If it's all about feelings, then I'm not going to fall for it. Trust me. I know what I'm talking about on this. If I just tell people, "Two thousand years ago, God became a baby, died to build us a Church, and now we eat Him," they would look at me like I looked at Jimmy's dad. So I have to be able to break it down and show why my statement is actually reasonable by using science, history, logic, philosophy, and the historical-critical method—not just emotion and warm fuzzies. You would be amazed at how many people look at me like a deer in the headlights when I ask them, "What evidence do you have to know that what you believe is actually true?"

Emma: Right. They start saying that it's their truth, etc., etc., leading us to pixies, gray wolves, and skydivers with no backpacks.

Sean: Yes!

Emma: And you are going to help me understand that believing in God and becoming a Christian is not pixie stuff. Right?

Sean: Yes I am, using faith and reason. We need to grow up intellectually, and eventually fairy tales need to end so that truth can make its way to the forefront of the mind. St. Paul explains it beautifully: "When I was a

36

child, I used to talk as a child, think as a child, reason as a child; when I became a man, I put aside childish things" (1 Corinthians 13:11).

Emma: Did you ask for a miracle or a sign?

Sean: Actually, no. Not everyone is converted by a miracle. I wanted knowledge.

Emma: So what you're saying is that reason is more important than signs.

Sean: No, they actually go hand in hand. God already gave us signs. If we can't find truth in those, then why would we believe in new ones? Jesus once healed ten lepers, but only one came back to say thank you. God made me with a rational mind, so I should be able to reason my way close enough to take a small leap of faith. I certainly understand there are some things that need to be bigger than my mind, otherwise God is not that big.

So if the evidence draws me to the conclusion that God exists, **the SECOND QUESTION to ask would logically be: "Then Who is He?"** Are you Allah? Buddha? Wiccan? High Power? Confucius? Jesus? I mean, there are many religions, so which one is right? Are they all right? Are they all wrong? They can't all be right if they contradict each other.

Emma: Is one of them actually right?

Sean: Some have more truth than others.

Emma: So there's some truth in all religions, but one has the fullness of truth?

Sean: Yes, they all can't be 100 percent right if they contradict each other. The Jews say Jesus wasn't God, but the Christians say He is. Can they both be right?

Emma: I guess not.

Sean: Guess not?

Emma: No, one is wrong or one is right.

Sean: Correct. That is a big one to get wrong. Either the Jews are missing something huge or the Christians are a bunch of idiots worshipping a 2,000-year-old dead guy who claimed to be God. We'll talk about it more, but see if this helps you for now.

Picture you have a child that you love greatly, and he is in the desert dying of thirst. You have four glasses of water. One is one-quarter full, one is one-half full, one is three-quarters full, and one is completely full. Which one would you want your child to drink?

Emma: The full one, of course.

Sean: Right. But is the one that is one-quarter full still good for your child?

Emma: Of course; it's water.

Sean: How about the one that is three-quarters full? Is that good?

Emma: Yes.

Sean: Then why did you pick the one filled to the top?

Emma: Because the glass filled to the top will help the child more. It will give him more water to quench his thirst.

Sean: And that's why I'm a Catholic. It is a faith that has more truth to quench my thirst. It has more ways of bestowing grace to quench my desire for holiness. It has more ways to quench my desire to know God more intimately.

Emma: Whoa, I get the concept, but you're still gonna have to prove that to me.

Sean: Excellent! Don't just take my word for it. Let's do some thinking and reason our way there. It is interesting to note that when I ask a room full of people if it matters to God what religion we are, almost all of them will say it does not. They have been conditioned through the years to think illogically. You see it today, even in Little League baseball. There are no winners. Everyone gets a trophy!

Now I'm not saying that God only loves people of certain religions. God loves us all. But it does matter to God which religion we are a part of. Satanism is a religion. It is the religion of hatred and total rejection of God. Do you think God would want you to be in that religion?

Emma: No, not at all.

Sean: Correct, so then does it matter to God what religion you are?

Emma: Wow, I guess it does.

Sean: See how we are using reason to discover truth?

Emma: Yes, it is interesting. It makes me wonder if there are any other ideas that I hold onto that I have not really looked at reasonably.

Sean: Congratulations, you are using your mind. All religions contain some truth, some more than others. Let me give the analogy of a dart board. The further away from the bull's-eye, the less truth that religion has. When you get to the bull's-eye, you've found the Catholic Church, and I want to explain why. But to be clear, I didn't just say that Hindus and Muslims and Protestants and Jews are evil, inferior people going to hell. I did NOT just say that.

Emma: I hear you. I know you did not condemn anyone. Why so emphatic about that?

Sean: Because, when truth exposes non-truth, non-truth fights back. But it can't fight with reason because there is no reason in non-truth, so non-truth has another tactic.

Emma: What is it?

Sean: Name-calling and lies. People who can't defend their position with reason and truth will attack the character of the person speaking the truth because they can't attack their argument. You see it all the time in politics, when the media will tear a person down by digging up dirt from the past to stop the truth the person is saying from coming out. It's a diversion, but it's very effective. People may ignorantly call me intolerant if I start showing why Christianity makes more sense than Buddhism. They can't use reason and logic to defend their position, so they try to label anyone who has dismantled their argument. They act out of fear instead of out of reason.

Emma: I definitely have done that myself. If a teacher calls me out and even I know I'm BS-ing, but don't want to give up the fight, I will attack her teaching skills or attack her character and intellect so I don't have to deal with the truth being laid on me.

Sean: We all struggle with that, but at least you're aware of it. You'll see it all the time now, especially with social issues. Keep your eyes open and judge a discussion by the content of the argument rather than the insults and the diversions.

What I want to do, Emma, is explain to you how reason compelled me to become Catholic. Why reason compelled me to leave Buddha. Did you know that many young adults are leaving Jesus for Buddha?

Emma: Why is that happening? Is it because he seems like a nice, happy guy?

Sean: Buddha says there is no God and all is illusion. Therefore truth is an illusion, and when there's no truth, you don't have to make truth statements, which means you don't have to take a stand. That way people won't be mad at you and you will always be liked.

Emma: And you don't have to feel guilty, either.

Sean: You don't have to feel guilty because everything's acceptable. Your truth is your truth, and their truth is their truth.

Emma: That sounds a bit like your friend who thought he could be a pixie when he died. That heaven is whatever you want it to be.

Sean: You've got it. But you see, Emma, there's a huge problem with Buddha's philosophy.

Emma: What?

Sean: Can't you see the problem of believing the statements, "All is illusion" and "There is no objective truth"?

Emma: What does *objective truth* even mean?

Sean: To say that a statement is "objectively true" means that it is true for people of all cultures, times, and places, even if they do not know it or recognize it to be true. Examples of this are: People need water and air to live. Or, water freezes once it is chilled to a certain temperature. *Subjective* truth, however, means that it's true for the person making the judgment, even though it may not be true for others. For example, saying: "It's freezing cold in here!" while others might be sweating.

Emma: Okay, got it. Now what's the problem with the statement that there is no truth?

Sean: Think about it. What question must we ask the person who says there is no truth? Come on, you can do this. Use your reason.

Emma: Oh man … I get it! The question I would ask is, "Is that statement true?" If someone says there is no truth, then they are making a truth statement! But if there is no truth, then even that statement isn't true! Right?!

Sean: Great job! Seriously, you have no idea how many people don't see this contradiction. So now tell me, what's wrong with saying, "All is illusion"?

Emma: I've got this. If all is illusion, then truth is illusion. And if truth is illusion, then how does the person know that what they're saying is true if that is an illusion, as well?

Sean: You are making me proud, girl.

Emma: Can you give me another teaching of Buddhism that's illogical? I do know Buddhists believe in god spirits, but not anything like the God of the Jews, Muslims, and Christians. They aren't really that important and are not the divine creator of the world, right?

Sean: Right. Buddha says that we all owe a great eternal debt and we can't be freed from ourselves until we pay it. You know that I respect science, and believe it is one of the powerful tools given to us to help us understand truth. That being said, here are the problems with that statement:

1. How can we owe an eternal debt if the universe is not eternal?
2. If there is no God, as Buddha says, then who do we owe this eternal debt to?
3. Who started the first "bad karma" that started the cycle of this debt in the first place? If the debt is eternal, we never actually find a first bad karma. We just keep going back for eternity, never reaching a starting point.
4. The object of Buddhism is to rid oneself of all desire because the Buddhist desires Nirvana. You must see the problem here.

Emma: I do! Wow, I never thought about it, but it jumps right out at you. How can a Buddhist reject all desire if his main **desire** is Nirvana? But what if Nirvana is something that just naturally happens from reaching enlightenment?

Sean: You used the word "reaching." If you are reaching for something, that means you desire it. There is no way around this. If a Buddhist obtains Nirvana, he "obtained" it, which means he captured it. Capturing is not at all letting go of something. Desire is at the core of Buddhism, while its followers are told not to desire.

Emma: Okay, I see some major flaws in this philosophy, but you still have a long way to go to convince me to be Catholic.

Sean: I wouldn't want it any other way. This way you will actually learn it. No short cuts!

Emma: So tell me the third question!

Sean: Okay, here it is. **The THIRD QUESTION is this: "What is the meaning of life?"** You know, why am I alive?

Emma: Really? I thought we were supposed to be traveling the world on a journey to find meaning like a mystical adventure, just like the movie *The Secret Life of Walter Mitty*!

Sean: It's a common misconception to think the meaning of life is to go on an adventure to find meaning. That is why you have millions upon millions of people going to secular book stores reading every self-help book in the world in an attempt to find meaning in their lives.

Emma: But shouldn't we all try to find meaning in the world?

Sean: No! You will not find fulfillment and meaning *in the world*. Look at yourself. You've been searching and experimenting with just about everything in the world. Have you found meaning in your life? When your friends are gone and you're not stoned and are sitting by yourself, are you happy? Do you feel safe? Is there peace inside you or are you always trying to escape?

Emma: No, I'm not happy, and that's why I'm here. I still have the buried demons that always creep back into my life. I was hoping that I would meet someone I could fall in love with who would help ease my pain, but every time I fall in love and everything is going fine, we eventually break up and I'm miserable because my one comfort is gone. I feel like I have to keep searching for Mr. Perfect—a guy who will never let me down—but I can't seem to find him.

Sean: There is only one who is perfect, and His name is God. You see, you're even using relationships to help fill that hole in your heart. The problem is that only God fits that hole in your heart. You're making a common, but enormous, mistake because you're using people to fill the void in your life. You're making them your "meaning," but people will always let you down because we are not God. We are NOT perfect.

Emma: So I should give up on finding love?

Sean: No, we can never give up on love—because we are loved by God. He did not leave us orphaned. He is seeking us out constantly, but again, He gave us free will to decide if we want to let Him into our hearts. The answer to the "meaning of life" question is that God created us so we could know Him, fall in love with Him, and spread that love to the world so that others can find Him through us. God wants us to fall in love with Him first. Then all the other relationships in our lives will be ordered.

Emma: What do you mean *ordered*?

Sean: Some of the most destructive things on the face of the earth are disordered relationships. I see it all the time. I see so many wounded people not in love with God who have fallen in love with each other and are using that relationship as ointment to cover the pain of the wounds hidden deep inside. Then when that relationship doesn't cover the wounds anymore, the breakup is devastating.

Emma: I think I'm guilty of that. Sean, I have even been so desperate for love that I've stayed with guys who have abused me.

Sean: I'm so sorry you've gone through that. Sadly, I see it a lot.

Emma: My parents are divorced. They said they fell out of love. How do I know I won't fall out of love if I ever find a great guy?

Sean: I don't buy the "falling out of love" notion. Love is a decision, not a feeling. Let's talk about marriage. If couples fall in love without God, it's very difficult for them to love their spouse as well as He intended them to. Many couples fall in love and look at each other with "goo-goo ga-ga" eyes, saying things like, "You complete me" or "You make life worth living." When I hear people talk like this, I think, "Man, are they in for an awakening!"

Because as time goes by, the "honeymoon" stage ends and the reality of bills, toilet seats, razor stubble, and work come into play. All of a sudden, one of the spouses isn't feeling "goo-goo ga-ga" anymore. They start to argue, saying, "You don't complete me anymore!" or "There is no more love and passion in you anymore!" One turns to work, the other to the Internet or sports, sitting on the couch oblivious to where his wife is while she reads books on "how to fix your husband." So they start to think they "fell out of love."

Trust me when I tell you that within every marriage there is a demon that has been buried and will reveal its fruit when the time is ripe. Sadly, some turn to another person so they can feel "goo-goo ga-ga" again. The problem is that those who do not learn from the past are doomed to repeat it. Statistics today reveal that in the U.S. 50 percent of first marriages, 67 percent of second marriages, and 73 percent of third marriages end in divorce.

Emma: Yeah, my dad left my mom and is now separated from his second wife. Please tell me there is hope for me. I don't want to be like them, but I'm starting to see that I'm acting more like my father every day.

Sean: There is always hope. Let me explain a better example of marriage for you. The healthiest marriage is when two people fall in love with God. When we do that, a couple of things happen.

1. We allow God to start working on our buried demons so we don't drag another creature into the marriage before we're healed. The Divine Physician starts to make a healthier person much more ready for marriage.
2. The person who loves God receives their joy and strength from God so they enter a marriage differently. Instead of looking at each other saying, "You complete me!" the couple can now say, "God completes me; now how can I serve you?" You see, it's dangerous to make the primary source of joy and fulfillment your spouse. No human being can fulfill that order. Christ helps us to look at our spouses not as objects to bring us joy, but as co-heirs in the kingdom of God—trying to help each other to grow in holiness and draw each other closer to Him. That makes for an

entirely different relationship: one that is centered on Christ and not centered on human beings.

Emma: That is beautiful. They both serve each other out of love because God first loved them.

Sean: Wow, that was spoken perfectly. You just quoted Scripture without knowing it. 1 John 4:19 says, "We love because He first loved us."

Emma: I want to be married like that. I love the part about how they want to serve each other and not just take from each other. It is such a perfect design. The men serve, as well?

Sean: Of course the men serve. Listen to what St. Paul says about it: "Husbands, love your wives, even as Christ loved the church and handed himself over for her to sanctify her, cleansing her by the bath of water with the word, that he might present to himself the church in splendor, without spot or wrinkle or any such thing, that she might be holy and without blemish. So [also] husbands should love their wives as their own bodies. He who loves his wife loves himself. For no one hates his own flesh but rather nourishes and cherishes it, even as Christ does the church" (Ephesians 5:25-29).

Emma: That is so powerful.

Sean: Do you know how Jesus gave Himself up for His Church? He served her and died for her. Jesus said, "… the Son of Man did not come to be served, but to serve, and to give his life as a ransom for many" (Matthew 20:28).

Emma: So God is asking men to be willing to die for their brides?

Sean: Yes, and so much more.

Emma: Okay, a couple of things here. First of all, I never knew the Bible had so much relatable stuff inside, and second, are there really men like that out there?

Sean: First, I agree that there is amazing "stuff" in the Bible. The Bible is the Word of God. God wrote you a book. You may want to read what He is telling you. Second, there *are* men like that out there, but to be honest, men of honor can be difficult to come by these days. But, how often have you been praying for men to be men of God? Have you been praying for your future spouse? Have you been praying that he will make good decisions now to help him from burying more demons? Now is a great time to be praying for all of those things. Third, men and women are not equal.

Emma: What? This is the first time you've lost me. I totally understand the first two things, but the third? Come on, man, I can't believe you just said that! Okay, why are you laughing?

Sean: Sorry, Emma, I set you up. I want to quote the philosopher and professor Dr. Peter Kreeft: "Men and women are not equal. Men are vastly superior to women at being men and women are vastly superior to men at being women." We are different, but we bring something beautiful to each other in this difference.

Emma: Oh man, I get it now. I thought you had become a jerk all of a sudden, and I almost lost faith in you.

Sean: Glad it makes sense. But don't put your faith in me; I will let you down. Put your faith in Jesus.

Emma: I'm not ready for that yet, but I am learning a lot, so keep going. No one has ever explained these things to me. It actually makes me kind of angry. If I had only known, I could have made better choices.

Sean: Remember, though, if I'm wrong about Jesus, then everything I'm telling you is just propaganda and you should disregard all of it. If Jesus is not God and did not rise from the dead, then putting your faith in Him is just as helpful as putting your faith in pixies and gray wolves. Don't just take my word for it. Listen to St. Paul in 1 Corinthians: "If Christ has not been raised, our preaching is useless and so is your faith."

Now, we certainly brought the third question of mine on a journey, but I want to make sure we come back to the root of the answer here. Remember that the meaning of life is not about man's attempt to find meaning. That is a cruel circular hoax. If our meaning is to search for meaning, that would mean if we found meaning, we'd have lost our meaning!

God already revealed to us why we were made. He wanted us to fall in love with Him and help others do the same. The meaning to life is … Jesus. We don't have to go searching all over the world to try to find Him. He is already searching for us. Not searching in the sense that He does not know where we are, but rather searching like a lover painfully waiting for the object of his affection to catch his gaze. We just need to let ourselves be found.

Emma: So God was lonely and made us so He could feel loved?

Sean: No, not at all. God is Trinity, one God in three Persons: the Father, the Son, and the Holy Spirit. He is perfectly content. God is perfection. God is Love, so He can't be lonely.

Emma: Then why did He make us?

Sean: So we could love and experience Him. There are times when I step outside and see an amazing sunset, and I go get my wife so she can see it, not for my sake, but for her sake. When I write her a song, I'm so excited for her to experience it because I know it's going to touch her heart in a beautiful way when she experiences it.

Emma: Right. Makes sense—if you're right, and there is a God. Because, if there's no God, there's no meaning to life.

Sean: Well, there is no ultimate objective meaning to life without God.

Emma: Please explain! This is going to be disturbing, isn't it?

Sean: Only disturbing if it were true that there is no God. But there *is* a God, so relax.

Chapter 5

Question 1: Does God Exist?

Sean: Okay, so let's get started. I'm going to share with you some evidence for the existence of God—not all of it because I would need to write another whole book just to list all that there is! People have already written those books, so, when I'm done, I'll give you the names of some great resources to read if you want to go further. Okay?

Emma: Sounds good. I am nervous, though.

Sean: Why?

Emma: Because I really want God to be real, but there has to be the evidence that you say there is for me to believe. I'm worried that if it turns out that there is no God, I'll be miserable forever.

Sean: Emma, let me ask you something.

Emma: What?

Sean: If there is no God and we prayed right now, would that hurt anything?

Emma: No, I guess not.

Sean: And if there *is* a God, then it could only help, right?

Emma: Yes, I suppose it would.

Sean: So let's pray. If there is no God, then we just wasted a little time. No big deal. But if there *is* a God, then we can ask for His help to open our hearts and minds. Cool?

Emma: Cool, but I don't know how to pray.

Sean: Of course you do. Just take all your worry and turn it into prayer. Tell God what you want.

Emma: I don't know, man …

Sean: Nothing to lose, right?

Emma: Why don't you pray for us this time?

Sean: I'm going to be teaching you a lot, and I need to know that you're committed. Remember that you should never try to teach the faith to someone who won't take it seriously. I always love to share the faith with those who are actually seeking—not to argue for the sake of arguing, but to talk with people who genuinely want to hear what I'm going to say. And I love hearing their thoughts, as well.

So, why don't you invest in the possibility that God may be there, and lead us in prayer. What do you want from God?

Emma: Okay … oh man … here goes. God, are you really there? If so, please let me know. I need to know! I don't want to be afraid anymore. Help me to believe if you are really there.

Sean: That was one of the most beautiful prayers I've ever heard.

Emma: Well, I meant it, but I felt like a fool.

Sean: You're not! And I want to point something else out to you, taking it a step further. Just like you have nothing to lose in saying a prayer, putting your faith in God can't hurt either. If He's not there, what have you lost? But if He *is* there ... then you gain everything.

Emma: Makes sense, but I still want to know that my faith is worth more than a gamble.

Sean: I love the way you're thinking now. The "can't lose betting on God" argument is true, but I also don't like just rolling the dice.

Emma: Right, so give me something I can hold onto that is real.

Sean: Fair enough. Let me use an illustration by the philosopher Richard Taylor. If we went on a journey through the desert and had been walking for weeks, seeing nothing but sand, then all of a sudden we came upon a basketball, what question would you ask?

Emma: I would ask, "How did that basketball get there?"

Sean: Right. And what if I answered you by saying, "It just is." Would that work for you as an answer?

Emma: Of course not.

Sean: Okay, now what if we walked further, and all of a sudden we saw a 20-foot-wide basketball in the sand? What question would you ask?

Emma: I'd once again ask, "How did that giant basketball get there?"

Sean: Yep. And if I said again, "It just is," does that work for you any better than it did the first time?

Emma: No, of course not. Giant basketballs don't just show up in the desert!

Sean: Okay, so let's turn the giant basketball into a giant universe. Look around. There is an amazing universe here. What questions are you going to ask?

Emma: How did the universe get here? Why is there a universe here?

Sean: It just is, Emma. Does that work for you?

Emma: No, it doesn't.

Sean: Exactly. There is a universe, but why is there a universe? Why is there *something* rather than *nothing*? Universes just don't pop into existence any more than giant basketballs do.

Emma: I totally get the point. But are you going to say that it's there because of God? I'm pretty sure that science has disproved God, my friend, so you will need a back-up plan.

Sean: Hmmm. Okay, so you think science has disproved God. I want to tell you about a debate I had a while ago with a science teacher. Let's call him Mr. Smith to protect his identity. Mr. Smith told one of the kids in my youth group that science had disproved God, and the teen was shaken up by this claim.

So I told the young man in my youth group to ask Mr. Smith if he was so certain about his statement that he wouldn't mind debating me in front of his class. The young man returned the next day with a message from Mr. Smith: "Bring it on."

Emma: He allowed you to come to his class?

Sean: Oh, much more than that. When I arrived two days later for this debate, he had opened it up for the entire school! We held it in the auditorium, and there were more than 500 ninth- to twelfth-grade students there, along with faculty. Mr. Smith said, "You wanted to debate, so if you know your stuff this should not bother you at all."

Emma: Were you freaked out?

Sean: No, not at all. Mr. Smith had no idea that the debate was over before it had even started.

Emma: Really? You were that confident?

Sean: Yes, even when I saw that Mr. Smith had a projector and video material for this debate. He was really ready with ammunition.

Emma: What happened? How long was it?

Sean: It was scheduled for an hour and thirty minutes, but it lasted only two minutes.

Emma: What? Why?

Sean: Because he had spoken ignorantly, and I was going to capitalize on that. So we were at our podiums, and I said in front of everyone, "Mr. Smith, I see you have brought videos and PowerPoint to help you win this debate tonight. But I have brought nothing but two questions. With these two questions, I can guarantee that the debate will be over in two minutes. I won't say anything else but my two questions, and you can have the hour and a half to yourself."

Emma: Did he accept?

Sean: He sure did because he wanted all that extra time to try to demolish me.

So I first asked, "Is it true you told a young man in my youth group that science had disproved God?" To which he responded, "You bet I did! Now you only have one question left!" I told him, "One question is all I really needed to begin with." For the first time, I sensed in him apprehension about my next question.

The second question I asked was this: "Can you scientifically demonstrate to me how science has disproved God?" He just stared at me. His eyes were blinking quickly, as his brain tried to compute a response, but the data banks were empty. It's like when you play chess with someone and checkmate him in four moves. He is still looking at the board, not aware that it's over.

So, he was staring and blinking, and I was starting to have fun, saying things like, "Come on, Mr. Smith, go get your Bunsen burner and beaker and scientifically show me how God does not exist!"

Emma: He couldn't.

Sean: No, he couldn't. He had made a really ridiculous and anti-scientific statement by saying science has disproven God. He looked at me, completely embarrassed, and said to everyone, "I misspoke." Emma, there is no scientific evidence that disproves God. You don't see chemists sitting in labs stirring beakers full of solutions, saying, "If we mix together some sodium and some iron, we can clearly see that God does not exist!"

Emma: Oh my gosh, you're right!

Sean: But you had fallen for that line yourself now, hadn't you?

Emma: Yes, but that was before I learned this new skill of being able to use reason! So how did it end?

Sean: He said, "What I meant to say is that we don't need God as an explanation of the universe!" I said, "I disagree, but that is an entirely different topic, and I would be glad to come back and debate you on that, as well. For now, I want the audience to be sure of what happened here today. Are you willing to admit before the school that there is no scientific evidence that disproves God?" And to his credit, he did.

Emma: I'm kind of embarrassed I bought into that line.

Sean: Remember that whenever someone makes a truth claim, we always have to ask the questions, "Is that true?" and "What evidence supports it?" It's really sad that people will try to use science as a weapon against God when without God we don't have science. That's like someone saying Leonardo da Vinci's Mona Lisa is proof that there was no Leonardo da Vinci. It's sad that some think science and religion are not compatible, when they actually synthesize nicely together.

Emma: But don't Christians believe the world is only 5,000 years old? I always hear that you guys are anti-science.

Sean: A lot of people speak ignorantly about the Church without having a clue as to what the Church actually teaches. Here is a great quote from Archbishop Fulton Sheen: "There are not more than 100 people in the world who truly hate the Catholic Church, but there are millions who hate what they perceive to be the Catholic Church."

Emma: If I am going to be fair, I must admit that I know nothing about the Catholic Church and have read nothing to see if the accusations made against it are true—and yet I still spread the gossip I have heard.

Sean: Wow, that is a powerful thing to realize. You've been intolerant and prejudiced against the Church. You've been "open-minded" to everything ... but the Church.

Emma: Ouch, that stings. But yes. That's true.

Sean: Let's set the record straight. The Church is not against science. The prestigious John Templeton Foundation honors achievements engaging the great questions of life and the universe. Have you ever heard of Michael Heller?

Emma: No.

Sean: He was the winner of the Templeton Prize on March 12, 2008. He is a Polish cosmologist and professor of philosophy at the Pontifical Academy of Theology in Krakow, Poland.

Emma: Sounds like a smart guy.

Sean: Yes, he is. He is also a Catholic priest.

Emma: What?!

Sean: Have you ever heard of the Big Bang Theory?

Emma: Of course, it was discovered by Albert Einstein.

Sean: Sorry, Emma. Wrong.

Emma: No way! It was Albert Einstein.

Sean: Actually, it was discovered by Father Georges Lemaître, who once said, "There is no conflict between religion and science." Einstein was skeptical of the Big Bang as a beginning to the universe.

Let me read some solid information to you from the Catholic Answers website: "The accepted idea in physics at the time was that the universe was essentially in a changeless state—a 'Steady State.' Where Einstein saw that the universe was actually moving—either shrinking or expanding— and devised the cosmological constant that maintained the stability of the universe, Lemaître concluded that the universe was expanding. Not only that, Lemaître proposed that from this it could be concluded that all matter and energy were concentrated at one point. Hence: The universe had a beginning.

"This theory, at first met with great skepticism, was termed rather sarcastically the 'Big Bang.' For his part, Lemaître elegantly described this beginning as 'a day without yesterday.' He presented his theory in January 1933 to a gathering of scientists in California, and at the end of his presentation, Einstein applauded and declared, 'This is the most beautiful and satisfactory explanation of creation to which I have ever listened.'

"Lemaître's ideas subsequently gained ground. Today, astrophysicists readily accept the Big Bang and the continuing expansion of the universe.

For his labors, Lemaître was made a member of the Royal Academy of Belgium and a canon of the cathedral of Malines. In 1936, Pope Pius XI inducted him into the Pontifical Academy of Science."

Emma: Are you serious? I never, ever heard of Lemaître! Why wouldn't someone tell us that?

Sean: That's another topic for another day. Now, have you ever heard of the Human Genome Project?

Emma: Never.

Sean: It's a complex multidisciplinary scientific enterprise directed at mapping and sequencing all of the human DNA and determining aspects of its function.

Emma: Uh, what?

Sean: I know, it sounds crazy. They mapped out the human DNA, and the head of this project is Francis Collins—one of the smartest men alive today, and he is a Christian. On Nov. 5, 2007, Collins received the Presidential Medal of Freedom, the nation's highest civil award, for his revolutionary contributions to genetic research.

Emma: Wow!

Sean: I'm not saying that because these men were Christians, that proves God is real. I'm just trying to let you see that brilliant people believe in God and that science and religion are not at odds with each other. If I didn't think it would bore you to death, I would give you a litany of all the Christians, Jews, and Muslims who have helped the advancement of science.

Emma: No need. I get the point.

Sean: Good. I'm glad you understand that concept because it's important. Now, we've asked the question, "Why is there a universe?" Let's see what the best explanation is. I am going to ask you some other questions, and I promise you they are not trick questions. They may seem like I am setting you up because the answers are very easy, but it is not to trick you.

Emma: Go for it.

Sean: Okay, imagine you are walking down the street and you come across a Rolex watch. You pick it up and see that it is beautiful, has many designs on it, and can tell time in many different countries. Which of these thoughts would you think?: A. *Wow, I can't believe this watch formed itself here out of nothing.* B. *Wow, this watch has existed for all eternity and no one made it.* C. *Wow, someone designed and put together a nice watch.*

Emma: Obviously C, someone designed it. It can't be A because watches can't form themselves out of nothing. It also can't be B because science tells us the universe is not eternal, therefore the watch just can't have existed forever.

Sean: Excellent! Great use of reason there! Now let's keep going with this. Next question: What is more complex, a Rolex watch or the entire universe?

Emma: Obviously the entire universe.

Sean: Very good. In fact, it is astronomically more complex than a watch. Now, do you know what the most complex object is in the universe?

Emma: Hmmm. Great question, give me a minute. I would say people.

Sean: Fantastic! Yes, our own DNA. Most people do not know that. So here is my question: How can you look at a Rolex watch and say, "Obviously someone designed and made this watch because it is so complex," and then look at our universe and our own DNA and say, "One big cosmic accident"?

Emma: You're right, that's crazy!

Sean: When we look at the universe, we see amazing design, and our DNA is just an unbelievable masterpiece.

Okay, Emma, so let's talk Big Bang. Thanks to Father Lemaître and the images from the Hubble telescope, science reveals to us that the universe had a beginning. Science also tells us that before the Big Bang there was no time, no space, and no energy. There was absolutely nothing.

Emma: That is such a difficult concept to grasp.

Sean: I know, it makes my head spin. But to be an atheist, Emma, you have to believe that out of nothing, something popped into existence by random chance. I think you must admit that's impossible. We know *ex nihilo nihil fit.*

Emma: Huh?

Sean: It's Latin for, "From nothing, nothing comes." Nothing can ever make anything because there is nothing there to *make* anything. Nothing has no properties. It is … nothing. Nothing is not a vacuum. It is not energy; it is nothing. Science tells us that every effect must have a cause. Effects don't just happen without a cause. Do you see this?

Emma: Actually, I do. But I have heard some scientists say that some things can come into existence out of nothing. Therefore, the universe could have.

Sean: Yes, I have heard that said also, but either the person saying that is a lousy scientist or a dishonest one. Some people will say that in the world of sub-atomic particles, "virtual particles" can come into existence out of nothing. This is really an insult and abuse to science. These theories come from the idea that particles can originate from fluctuations of energy from within a vacuum. Unfortunately for lay people, when they hear the term vacuum, they think it means "nothing," when in actuality a vacuum is a sea of fluctuating energy governed by physical laws and having physical structure. People who profess the "something from nothing" theory are unable to distinguish "nothing" from empty space. Nothing is not empty space! Nothing is the absence of anything at all—*including* space itself!

Also, if things like the universe just popped into existence, why don't we see that happening all the time? If it's true about the universe, then we should be seeing all kinds of strange things happening. You would be walking down the road, and all of a sudden an elephant would pop up in front of you! We never see this, yet people want to believe that it can happen with a *universe*? Come on, let's be reasonable here, folks.

Emma: Wow, I totally understood what you just said. I never understood the reality of "nothing" before. In light of that, I do see that it is ridiculous to claim that something came from nothing. It is actually comical now to think about it. Nothing comes from nothing.

Sean: Excellent! The problem is that when trying to explain difficult concepts to lay people, scientists use analogies that are not sufficient and can distort the truth of the actual science. Just because there is a program on TV with a scientist speaking does not mean it's true, so we need to be careful what we swallow when watching TV or reading.

Emma: Okay, but what if the universe has *always* existed?

Sean: Well, a couple of things. First, the overwhelming scientific data tells us that the universe is not infinite. I'm going to use a big word here, so don't let it scare you off from listening. You'll understand this. I want to teach you about the Second Law of Thermodynamics.

Emma: Okay. I have heard of it, but I don't know what it really is.

Sean: The Second Law of Thermodynamics states that matter and energy always tend towards disorder—a concept scientists call *entropy*. The illustration of a pool cue is often used to help explain this. When a pool cue hits a racked table, the balls go flying about wildly. They never come back into the racked position, and eventually the energy dies and they slowly come to a halt. According to the Second Law, things go from order to disorder, like the balls on the pool table. In addition, the Second Law teaches that all things—including heat and energy—go to equilibrium. When you hold a plate of hot food in a room, the food eventually gets colder and the room gets warmer until they are the same temperature. This is going to happen to the universe, as well. All of the stars are going to eventually cool and die. This is what scientists call "heat death."

Emma: Sounds depressing.

Sean: I know, but this will help you understand why we can know the universe is not infinitely old.

Emma: Wait, I think maybe I get it.

Sean: Go for it.

Emma: If the universe is eternal, it should have used up all of its energy by now. Heat death should have already occurred, but it hasn't.

Sean: You are amazing! Well done. Remember also, just like the pool balls on the pool table, the universe should have just scattered randomly, but it didn't. It became very organized. You see, if God doesn't save us, the universe is going to grow cold and dead. And if the universe were eternal, it would have already died. With the creation of the Hubble telescope, we were also able to see that galaxies were traveling away from each other at amazing speed from the beginning of time.

Emma: So all the galaxies are traveling away from each other into space?

Sean: Not exactly. Space itself is expanding. The philosopher William Lane Craig uses this great visual to help us understand it more clearly: Imagine a balloon with buttons attached to the outside of it. The buttons represent the galaxies and the balloon is space itself. As we inflate the balloon, the skin of the balloon is expanding the buttons away from each other. Likewise, space itself is expanding the galaxies from each other.

Then in 1965, a discovery was made. Cosmic Microwave Background Radiation was discovered. Those are particles from the original Big Bang that have turned into microwaves. Evidence like this has sealed the fate of the static universe. The universe had a beginning! Virtually all scientists agree with this. There are a few on the fringe who want to fight this, and there is a reason why. Can you guess?

Emma: I think I can. When someone goes against such overwhelming evidence, they have an agenda. So maybe the reality of the Big Bang means that the universe needed a cause ... which leads us to the possibility of God. And those scientists don't want that.

Sean: You nailed it. Now let's keep going. Say you were in the kitchen and you heard a "Bang!" in the living room. You asked me what made that bang, and I said, "Nothing, there was just a bang." What would you think?

Emma: That you are a liar.

Sean: Exactly, so now figure out where I'm going with this.

Emma: It's like the basketball in the desert. The bang can't just bang—someone needs to bang it. Therefore, if there were a big bang that started the whole universe, someone had to make that bang.

Sean: You are going to be an amazing witness of the faith when you convert!

Emma: Oh man, not so fast!

Sean: I also notice that you said "someone," not "something," had to make the bang. You're correct that it had to be someone and not something. If time, space, matter, and energy came into being at the Big Bang, then whatever caused the Big Bang must have been something that is without matter and energy—something spaceless and timeless. There are only two possibilities that fit that definition. The first possibility is an abstract thing, such as a number. The second possibility is a spirit. We know that numbers do not think, so they cannot choose to create. Therefore, the only thing we are left with is a spirit that is incomprehensibly powerful.

Emma: I get it. It had to be someone that made the decision to create. Only things with minds can choose.

Sean: You have no idea how well you are comprehending all of this information. Since you are mastering all of this, it's time for another new term.

Emma: Last one was easy, so lay it on me.

Sean: That's the spirit! Okay here it is: The Kalam Cosmological Argument. It was framed out by a twelfth-century Muslim theologian named Al-Ghazali. William Lane Craig has brought the Kalam Cosmological Argument to the front lines of the God debate. He states it like this:

1. Whatever begins to exist must have a cause.
2. The universe began to exist.
3. Therefore, the universe has a cause for its existence.

Read it three times, Emma. You need to memorize it. I wrote it down for you here.

Emma: 1. Whatever begins to exist must have a cause. 2. The universe began to exist. 3. Therefore, the universe has a cause for its existence. Perfectly logical.

Sean: It's airtight unless you try to disprove the first premise, which says everything that begins to exist must have a cause. Good luck with that one! Premise two states that the universe began to exist. Now again, there are some people way out there who claim that the universe did not begin to exist, but is eternal. Science has debunked that, and it makes no sense philosophically, either.

Emma: What do you mean?

Sean: Let me take an example from Trent Horn's book, *Answering Atheism*: Imagine your aunt works in a flower store, and every day before work she has to count all the flowers in her shop before she opens up the shop. If she had 12 flowers, she would open fairly quickly, but if she had a million, it would take quite a while for her to open. Now imagine she had an infinite number of flowers. How long would it take her before she could open her store?

Emma: She never could. There would always be another flower to count, and she would never finish counting them.

Sean: So what is the problem here if the universe is infinitely old?

Emma: With the flower shop, my aunt never opens the door because she is infinitely counting the flowers. With the universe, if it is infinite, there would always be one more day before this one, so this day would never come. WE would never be able to "open the door" to today. Yet this day has come, so the universe can't be infinite.

Sean: Honestly, Emma, you are picking this all up quicker than I did.

Emma: It feels like a switch that has been off for a while has been turned on in my brain. I like the Kalam formula. It is foolproof in my book, but there is a problem with it that I just thought about. If everything that exists has a cause … then if God exists, He, too, needs a cause.

Sean: Okay, you need to look at the first premise one more time. It does not say that anything that exists must have a cause. It says that anything that **begins** to exist must have a cause. God did not **begin** to exist. He is eternal and necessary.

Emma: Okay, hang on. I'm going to need some help with this one.

Sean: Believe it or not, it's not that complicated. You are asking the question, "If God made everything, then who or what made God?"

Emma: Right.

Sean: I know if I gave you enough time you could figure this all out on your own, but I am going to jump-start this for you. Okay, let's review. Science tells us that time began when?

Emma: With the Big Bang.

Sean: Right, so that tells us God is outside of time. This is a concept that makes your head spin, but if time did not exist before the Big Bang, then obviously God is outside of time, making Him what?

Emma: Timeless … whoa … that's crazy.

Sean: It is amazing to think about, but it's true. Therefore if God is outside of time, does He have a beginning?

Emma: No! I get this! Beginnings deal with time, and there is no time where God is because He is outside of time. Therefore He doesn't begin or end; He just is! Right?

Sean: You set this up perfectly, Emma. And you're leading us to Scripture again.

Emma: How?

Sean: When Moses went to the burning bush to speak with God, he asked God a question. Look here at Exodus 3:13-14: "Then Moses said to God, 'If I go to the Israelites and I say to them, 'The God of your ancestors has sent me to you,' and they ask me, 'What is His name?' What do I tell them?' God replied to Moses, 'I AM WHO I AM.' Then He added: 'This is what you will tell the Israelites: 'I AM has sent me to you.'"

God is the greatest conceivable being, absolute perfection. Therefore, nothing could have created God because cause and effect tells us that the effect can never be greater than the cause. If something created God, that cause would be greater than God because God would then be the effect. Follow?

Emma: But why couldn't a greater God be the cause of that God?

Sean: Let's think about this. If some God created God, then another God would have to create that God, and so on and so on—but it can't go on infinitely. Remember the previous example I used about your aunt owning a flower shop and having to count to infinity before she could open it up? Let's apply the same principle here for an infinite regression of Gods.

Close your eyes. I want you to picture the image of a domino in your mind right now. Picture it on the ground, standing upright. Attached to the front of it is an explosive, and when that domino tips over, that explosion will start the universe. Got it?

Emma: Got it.

Sean: So now we have one domino standing upright. We are going to need another domino right behind that one so that when it flips over, it will knock over the domino that will cause the Big Bang. However, we are now going to need another domino that will knock over that domino that will knock over the domino that will cause the Big Bang. You see where this is leading, I hope.

Emma: I do! The dominoes can't go back infinitely. There has to be one domino powerful enough to *move itself*. If we have an infinite regression, we will never get to the present! The God domino that will cause the Big Bang will never flip over because if the past is infinite we never arrive at the present! Like my aunt, if she can't open the store until she counts all the flowers and there is an infinite number of flowers, the store never opens. In the same way, if there were an infinite number of Gods going back infinitely, the universe never would have begun! The God domino would never have flipped over. But the God domino *did* flip over because we know there was a Big Bang! Oh, my head: I actually get this.

Sean: Let me share an example that William Lane Craig uses: You ask to borrow five dollars from me, and I say, "Sure, no problem," but I don't have the money on me, so I'm going to borrow it from Jeff. But Jeff says he will have to borrow it from Erin, and Erin says she will borrow it from Frank. If this goes on infinitely, will you ever get your five dollars?

Emma: No, I never will. An infinite past means no finish line.

Sean: Yes! Isn't it awesome? I love this stuff. So, to review, we now know a couple of things: The universe began to exist, and the God domino moved and started the Big Bang. So what does that tell us about the God domino—or God—if we can't have an infinite regression of Gods?

Emma: It tells us that God had to always exist. If God did not always exist under His own power, then we have an infinite regression of Gods, meaning nothing ever started—but something did start! The universe did not create itself because that is impossible. Something had to create it. Everything that begins to exist like the universe must have a cause because science tells us the universe began to exist. God, however, did not Himself begin to exist. He is spaceless and timeless.

Sean: And necessary. The uncaused cause (God) started it all, and this cause had to choose to do it and had to be powerful.

Emma: The uncaused cause that is spaceless, timeless, and all-powerful ... God.

Sean: God, indeed. I noticed something amazing, Emma. Not only did you call God timeless, but also spaceless!

Emma: Well, if space and time did not begin until the Big Bang, then we know God has to be not only timeless, but spaceless. Let me say this all again, so I don't lose it ...

1. We know the universe began to exist. Science tells us this. The Hubble telescope reveals that the universe is traveling away at amazing speed, and the discovery of the background radiation from the Big Bang tells us that at some point the universe began to exist.
2. The universe is not eternal. The Second Law of Thermodynamics explains that if the universe were eternal, it would have used up all of its energy by now, resulting in heat death.

3. The Kalam Cosmological Argument states that anything that begins to exist must have a cause. The universe began to exist. Therefore, the universe must have a cause.

4. Whenever you see order and design, there is always a designer—like with the Rolex watch. If someone had to design a watch, someone definitely had to design the universe and our own DNA.

5. The universe cannot create itself because that is completely illogical. The universe is the effect, and something caused that effect. Cause and effect! How did I miss that? Just as I cannot create myself, the universe can't cause itself!

6. Whatever caused the universe must be outside of space and time because science reveals that space and time did not begin until the Big Bang. The cause must also have a mind because it *chose* to create, and the cause must also be powerful beyond our comprehension to create the universe out of nothing! This is amazing to me right now. I get this, Sean!

Sean: Let me add to your amazement of God. It is actually not correct to say that God created something out of nothing. That lends us to see "nothing" as something used for the formation of the universe—and we have to be careful because it will give that false impression that nothing is something. God did not hold "nothing" in His hand and make something. God brought about "something" by His will.

"Men, indeed, are not able to make something from nothing, but only from existing material. God, however, is greater than men first of all in this: that when nothing existed beforehand, he called into existence the very material for his creation" (St. Irenaeus, Against Heresies 2:10:4 [A.D. 189]).

Emma: Yes, that is even more amazing! This Irenaeus guy already knew this 2,000 years ago?

Sean: This Church would amaze the whole world if people would only read. Now, let's touch a little more on the evidence from design. Scientists refer to it as the fine-tuning of the universe. I want you to see just how special the universe really is with a piece from William Lane Craig's awesome book called, *On Guard—Defending Your Faith with Reason and Precision.*

Basically what he says is that physicists are amazed at the complexity and fine tuning of the universe. Any tiny change to this balance, and we do not have a life-permitting universe. Let me give you some crazy numbers, just so you can see the amazing magnitude of this:

The number of seconds in the entire history of the universe is around 10^{17} power. That's a one followed by 17 zeros. 100,000,000,000,000,000. The number of subatomic particles in the entire known universe is said to be around 10^{80} power. That is a one with 80 zeros after it. These numbers are so massive, they are really incomprehensible to us. If we changed that value by even ONE part of 10^{100} power, our universe could simply not have supported life.

Let me quote directly now from Craig's work: "Now with those numbers in mind, consider the following examples of fine tuning. The so-called *weak force* of the four fundamental forces of nature, which operates inside the nucleus of an atom, is so finely tuned that an alteration in its value by even one part of 10^{100} power would have prevented a life-permitting universe!" He continues to say that a change in the *cosmological constant,* which drives the acceleration of the universe's expansion, by as little as one part in 10^{120} power, would also have resulted in a life-prohibiting universe.

Emma: Okay, I am a little lost with some of the wording, but it is clear that these numbers are huge, and if they changed at all ... we would not be here.

Sean: Exactly. We just happen to have the perfect numbers (that are astronomical) for a life-permitting universe. Sound like more than a coincidence?

Emma: Absolutely.

Sean: Let's see if this analogy helps you, as well: Imagine if I took one trillion decks of cards and stacked them together in a pile, then put a nuclear bomb in the middle of the pile. You go away and come back a week later, and there is a giant shopping mall made entirely of the trillion decks of cards. You ask me how I made it, and I tell you that I blew them up with a bomb and they fell together like that. Would you believe me?

Emma: Ha, of course not.

Sean: What if I tried it every day for a trillion years. Would that explosion ever make a mall out of cards?

Emma: No way.

Sean: Well, the odds of a life-permitting universe forming are vastly more improbable than the example of a card mall forming from a bomb exploding. So if a mall of cards can't be created by an explosion, then why would we believe that it would happen to a universe? Unless, of course someone fine-tuned that explosion and directed everything.

Think about this, Emma: To be an atheist, you have to believe that out of nothing something popped into existence, exploded, and became more complex, then life from non-life came about, and that life became so complex that it can create symphonies … all by random chance!

Emma: That's ridiculous. I see that now.

Sean: Correct. Believing *that*, my friend, would take a lot of "blind faith." The scientific evidence is clearly behind the idea of a Creator. Now let's find out who He is.

Chapter 6

Question 2: Then Who Is He?

Emma: Okay, so I see that the evidence leads us to believe there is a God or that at least faith in God is reasonable. That being said, it brings us to the second of the three questions now. Am I right?

Sean: You bet. Now Emma, I'm going to take for granted that you believe Jesus was a historical person. Virtually all historians agree on this because of the overwhelming historical evidence.

Emma: No problem, I believe that He walked the earth.

Sean: Good! Now back to the question at hand: "If there is a God, then who is He—Buddha, Jesus, Muhammad, Confucius, etc.?"

Emma: And they can't all be right because they teach different things, right?

Sean: Yes, they teach things that contradict each other. Would a loving God contradict Himself?

Emma: No, that would cause confusion, and only a sick and twisted god would cause confusion over who he is.

Sean: You've got it. But, sadly, many people don't. I once had a woman come up to me when I was in the middle of a friendly debate with a Buddhist and say, "Why can't you guys just get along? You all worship the same God, only differently!" Whenever I hear people talk like this, I cringe. First of all, they assume that a debate is a bad thing. Second, their lack of understanding of world religions is sad. I have at least taken the time to read about and speak with people of other faiths and philosophies to get a good grasp of what they are all about. This woman insulted all religions by basically saying, "All that crap you guys do and profess isn't important because you all worship the same God anyway."

Emma: Basically, what this woman said was that she claims to know the truth about God herself while belittling all religions. She was actually being really arrogant.

Sean: Exactly. Arrogant and ignorant. Every once in a while, I'll get together with some friends who are Jewish, Muslim, Buddhist, and Hindu, and we talk, challenge, and debate each other. Then we go out to eat and have a couple of drinks. I would LOVE to have that woman show up while we were all together and say that we all worship the same God. My friends would destroy her statement and put her in her place.

Emma: What would they say?

Sean: Well, my Jewish friend would say, "Same God? The Christians believe Jesus is God, but we do not!" My Buddhist friend would say, "Honey, you are mistaken ... there is no God!" My Hindu friend would say, "You poor thing ... you are God." And my Muslim friend would say, "Jesus was not God, and we disagree with the Christians. Muhammad was the final prophet—and besides ... who has given you such knowledge as to arrogantly profess that you know more than all the world religions?"

Emma: Wow, that would take her back a bit.

Sean: Yes. Not everyone worships the same God. Hindus look at a cow and see divinity, whereas I look at a cow and see a steak. Christians, Muslims, and Jews do worship the same God, but the Jews have yet to accept Jesus as the Son of God Emmanuel ("God is with us"), so they are missing the fullness of God's revelation. The same goes for the Muslims; they are right in saying there is one God, but after that things get really off-track.

Let the late great St. John Paul II explain it here from his work *Crossing the Threshold of Hope*: "Whoever knows the Old and New Testaments, and then reads the Koran, clearly sees the process by which it completely reduces Divine Revelation. It is impossible not to note the movement away from what God said about Himself, first in the Old Testament through the Prophets, and then finally in the New Testament through His Son. In Islam, all the richness of God's self-revelation, which constitutes the heritage of the Old and New Testaments, has definitely been set aside. Some of the most beautiful names in the human language are given to the God of the Koran, but He is ultimately a God outside of the World, a God who is only Majesty, never Emmanuel, God-with-us. Islam is not a religion of redemption. There is no room for the Cross and the Resurrection" (p. 92).

Islam unfortunately sets our understanding of God's love back 5,000 years because it denies God's sacrifice on the cross for us. In Islam, God is not loving father but, rather, master.

All religions contain some truth—even Satanism. It has one truth … Satan is real. As I mentioned earlier, you can think of religions as a dartboard. The further away from the bullseye you get, the less truth that religion has. When you get to the bullseye, you have the Catholic Church.

Emma: Bold statement.

Sean: Yes, it is. But remember, I'm not calling people of other religions evil or saying they're going to hell. I'm not judging people. I'm simply asking logical questions about their faith claims to see if they are logical, just as I did when I was exploring Catholicism.

Emma: Like you said earlier, when people do that, they attack you instead of the argument. It's a diversion.

Sean: Good! Now keep that in mind when we talk. Christians don't spread the word of Jesus because we think we're better than anyone else. We actually want the world to know the awesome love of Jesus. Imagine you're sick in bed and using a certain medicine that brings you a little bit of comfort, but I show up with a different medicine that not only makes you feel better, but cures you. Would you be mad at me for bringing it over?

Emma: I would love you for it!

Sean: That's all I'm trying to do here, Emma. The problem is that some people love their medicine so much—because they've been using it for so long—that they have a hard time trying something new, even if it's better for them.

Emma: That's my mother to a T. But I can see how it would put people off if you were to claim that your medicine (religion) is "better" than someone else's.

Sean: Agreed. That's why when Christians speak about the faith, it must be done with sincere love and charity. Emma, I'm not trying to sell you a product so I can prove a point or manipulate you into thinking as I do. I am genuinely excited for you to encounter Jesus. Just as I want my wife with me when I see a sunrise, I also want you to experience the fullness of God's love through Jesus.

Again, If there is no God, then by all means believe whatever you want because there is no ultimate meaning to life anyhow and we have no souls and are just robots. Have fun. But if God exists, then He may have a name and a message.

Emma: I once heard the analogy about people being blindfolded. Each touches one part of an elephant and assumes that elephants are only like the part they touched. Isn't that like all the world religions? They each only have a piece of God?

Sean: I know the story: A number of blind men came to an elephant. Somebody told them that it was an elephant. The blind men asked, "What is the elephant like?" As they started to touch the elephant, one man, while touching its leg, said that it was like a thick tree. Another man, touching its ears, said that it was like a flag. And one man, holding its trunk, said it was like a snake.

What this story is trying to say is that all the blind men miss the true nature of reality because they take their limited perspective to be the total picture. But we can "see" that they're all missing the point. If they would just listen to one another with humility and respect, accepting each person's experience as equally valid, then they would be able to arrive at a more accurate understanding.

Emma: Sounds pretty good, but I have a feeling you are going to show me why this is illogical, aren't you.

Sean: Yep! Actually I am going to let Clay Jones, associate professor of Christian Apologetics at Biola University, explain it. He wrote on his blog:

"First, these guys are obviously not the sharpest burritos in the hallway! You'd have to be a pretty ignorant blind man to grab hold of the first thing you touched and feel no further when the whole purpose of being there was because you wanted to find out what an elephant was like. Wouldn't they, as they kept feeling the beast, be able to come up with a pretty good understanding of an elephant? Not only that, while they were arguing, each of them could have brought the others over to the part that they had first felt and then they would all change their minds as to what an elephant was like.

Second, notice in the story that there is one person who isn't blind—the storyteller. The storyteller knows that the blind men are feeling an elephant and what an elephant really looks like because he, as the storyteller, isn't blind. Thus the storyteller is able to judge that all the blind men are 'partly right' but 'mostly wrong.' Likewise, those who tell us that no one really knows what God is like, and that all of us might be somewhat right and somewhat wrong, put themselves in a position similar to the storyteller. But what gives them the right to be storyteller? How is it that they see things so clearly as to know that everyone else's claims are mistaken?

Third, contrary to the unseen elephant, Christianity is based on the testimony of those who said they did see God and then told us about what they saw. After all, Jesus said, 'He who has seen me has seen the Father' (John 14:9), and 'I and the Father are one' (John 10:30). Thus John wrote, 'That which was from the beginning, which we have heard, which we have seen with our eyes, which we looked upon and have touched with our hands, concerning the word of life—the life was made manifest, and we have seen it, and testify to it and proclaim to you the eternal life, which was with the Father and was made manifest to us' (1 John 1:1-2)."

Emma: So that basically dismantles that analogy!

Sean: Jesus changes everything. He made claims that no others made, and we have to see if they are true. One of the saddest things I see happening with young people and even their parents is their lack of understanding of who Jesus is. When leading a retreat, I'll ask a group of people if they believe in Jesus. All the hands go up. Then I ask how many of them believe Jesus is God. Only 20 percent of the hands go up. I then ask them how many believe that Jesus was not God but rather sent by God to teach us how to love. Almost all of the hands go up.

Emma: And that's wrong?

Sean: Yes, that's wrong! Jesus is God! Not a nice teacher or enlightened soul. No offense, but that is ridiculous.

Jesus claimed to be God. His life, death, and resurrection proved it. Remember, here are some of Jesus' own words: "I and the Father are one," "I am the Way, the Truth and the Life," "Everyone who lives in me and believes in me will never ever die," "Unless you eat my flesh and drink my blood you have no life in you." Emma, if I went around your neighborhood saying those things, would you let me play with your children one day?

Emma: Oh my, no!

Sean: Why not?

Emma: Because I would think you were crazy.

Sean: Exactly! If someone claims to be God and he is not, then we should not worship him. We should send him to an institution for the mentally troubled. As the great C.S Lewis wrote, Jesus was either a liar, a lunatic, or God. There's no way around it. He can't be a nice, enlightened soul, if He thinks He is God but is not. Remember that Jesus referred to himself as "I Am." Do you remember whose name that is?

Emma: I do. It is Yahweh, I Am who Am. It is God's name. The uncaused cause of the universe.

Sean: Good job. That name was not to be spoken because it was so holy. Jesus called Himself "I Am!" "Amen, amen I say to you, before Abraham came to be, I AM (John 8:58)." Do you know the story of doubting Thomas?

Emma: He was one of the apostles who did not believe Jesus rose and would not believe unless he could put his finger in the hole in Jesus' side from where he was stabbed by the centurion's spear.

Sean: Sometimes I think you know way more than you let on, but yes, that is the story. Jesus appeared to Thomas and told Him to touch his side. Scripture does not say he did touch it, but it does say that when he saw Jesus and the wounds, he said, "My Lord and my God." Now, Jesus did not rebuke him for calling Him God. He allowed it. He allowed Himself to be worshipped because if He is God, then it is deserved. But if He is not God, then He is either evil or insane.

Emma: Okay, I get it. They can't have it both ways. Either He's a madman or God—but no enlightened teacher or spiritual guru. So then, you are saying Jesus is God.

Sean: No, Jesus Himself is saying He is God. God is Trinity. Three Persons in one God: God the Father, God the Son, and God the Holy Spirit. There are not three Gods. The Trinity is a great mystery, but it is logical.

See if you can picture this: God the Father, who is eternal, gives Himself totally and completely to the Son, who is also eternal, and the Son reflects that love back to the Father. That love between them is the Holy Spirit. Listen to what Pope Francis spoke about the Trinity: "The light of Easter and Pentecost have renewed in us each year the joy and wonder of faith that recognizes that God is not something vague, abstract, but has a name: 'God is love.'" And this love "is not sentimental, emotional, but the love of the Father who is the source of all life, the love of the Son who died on the cross and rose, the love of the Spirit who renews man and the world."

He continued to say that the Trinity "is not the product of human reasoning, it is the face which God Himself revealed, not from the top of a throne, but walking with humanity in the history of the people of Israel, and above all in Jesus of Nazareth. Jesus is the Son who made us know the merciful Father and brought to the world His 'fire,' the Holy Spirit."

Emma: Wow, that is so beautiful!

Sean: I don't want to get bogged down too much in explaining more of the Trinity. The point being made is that Jesus is fully God—not part of God or just some ambassador.

But—and this is really important, too—while He is fully God, He's also fully man.

Emma: Huh?

Sean: Let's see if another analogy helps here.

I took my niece fishing one day. The fishing was amazing, but after about three hours, my little niece was crying. I asked her what was wrong, and she told me she was starving ... because I had forgotten to feed her.

Emma: That's so sad!

Sean: I know, I know, but I redeemed myself. I told her I would make a sandwich for her. I turned to the picnic table and started making a sandwich, but I started hearing her grunt over and over again. I turned to see that she was carrying a bucket over to the table, and it seemed heavy. I asked her what was in it … just as she dumped out a huge snapping turtle onto the picnic table!

Emma: No way!

Sean: Yeah! I was freaked, so I took my walking stick and knocked the thing off the table.

Emma: You are a sad man.

Sean: Hey, it was near my sandwich! Anyway, when it hit the ground, it was upside down. My niece cried and told me to go turn it over. Do you know that snapping turtles hiss? I ran into the woods to get a bigger stick!

When I came back from the woods, my niece had her hands out, praying to God, saying, "Make me a turtle! Make me a turtle!" I asked her what she was doing, and she looked at me impatiently and said, "You are sooo stupid. If God makes me a turtle, then I can speak with *this* turtle and tell him not to be afraid. And we can turn him over so you can stop hitting him with sticks!"

Emma: That is hilarious!

Sean: I know, pretty funny, but I must admit it is also a great teaching moment. Tell me: If my niece wants to talk to a turtle, what must she become?

Emma: A turtle?

Sean: Correct. Now If God is a spirit but wants to talk to a human, hug a human, walk with a human, and dine with a human, what would He become?

Emma: A human?

Sean: That's right. And He did that in the Person of whom?

Emma: Jesus! This is the first time in my life I actually understand that concept. Jesus would have to become one of us in order to communicate with us and love us best. So He did. He is God in the flesh.

Sean: Yes, Jesus is God in the flesh, fully God and fully man at the same time. Jesus' claims were absolutely radical and completely different than that of Buddha, Muhammad, and Confucius. Buddha said, "Follow my way." Confucius said, "Follow my path." And Muhammad said, "Follow my doctrine." But Jesus said, "Follow *me*." Buddha said that his teachings would lead to the door, but Jesus said, "I *am* the door." Jesus desires us to follow ***Him*** and worship ***Him***!

Emma: Okay, I see that. Totally different teachings. Buddha is asking people to follow a philosophy, but Jesus actually wants us to worship *Him*. He *is* the path; He *is* the door.

Sean: Right! Jesus said, "I am the way and the truth and the life. No one comes to the Father except through me" (John 14:6).

Emma: And, in order to help us follow Him, He became man.

Sean: Yes. Fully God and fully man. Dying on a cross for the forgiveness of sins, opening the gates of heaven, and building us a Church.

Chapter 7

Oh, How He Loves Us

Sean: You know, Emma, I think now is a good time to tell you why I decided to leave Buddha to follow Jesus. Before I really came to Christianity, what I practiced was being a "spiritual" person.

Emma: What does that mean?

Sean: It means I believed in the spiritual world and that we are more than energy and matter. I believed there was a God, but I did not belong to a religion. Being "spiritual" allows you to believe in God, but you get to create Him the way *you* want Him to be. It's like Build-a-Bear.

Emma: What?

Sean: Yeah, you know, like at the store where you build your own stuffed animals, you get to stuff God with what you want and leave out what you don't want: "My God loves drugs and promiscuity, and I call him George!" Sorry, couldn't resist. Basically, being "spiritual" without religion means that you get to decide who God is for you.

Emma: Okay, that doesn't make sense to me at all. Shouldn't we first find out who God is, then become who He wants us to be ... instead of just making God who we want *Him* to be?

Sean: I love it! Yes, in fact, the "spiritual" person becomes the creator of God by making God in his image and likeness instead of living the reality that God made *us* in His image and likeness.

Emma: How can someone not see that?

Sean: People can easily fall for deceptions that sound good when spoken, until they really take a look at them and use their reason.

Emma: Can you give me an example?

Sean: I have the perfect one for you. There was a girl who every day would post a Facebook message that said, "Everyone needs to follow their own heart!" Every day she would post the same thing, and she would get thousands of responses, like, "You touched my heart!" or "That's so beautiful and true." Want to know what I posted?

Emma: Oh no …

Sean: I posted, "That's what Hitler did!"

Emma: No, you didn't!

Sean: Of course I did. Trust me, Emma, you do not want everyone following their own hearts. What if a guy wakes up saying, "My heart wants me to kill Emma"? Do you want him following his heart?

Emma: No!

Sean: I don't want to follow my own heart. When I do that … I sin. I want to follow the heart of God. The question is, "Is His heart knowable?" The answer is, "Yes." You see, Emma, people who are "spiritual" with no religion don't realize this, but more often than not they are actually not being led by God but rather by buried demons.

Emma: The wounds of our past that we bury.

Sean: Yes. For example, the man who feels scared of commitment because of some past wounds may create a God who says having sex with multiple partners is okay. Or the guy who is really lazy may create a God who says you don't have to go to church.

Emma: I can see how people would do that. So that's what you did?

Sean: Yes, I was great at making up a God who didn't care what I did because I was a "good" person. So one time I was speaking at a college about "spirituality," saying all kinds of things that sound great but in reality are ridiculous. I would tell people things like, "It doesn't matter what you believe, just be sincere in your belief," which is stupid. Sounds just like my friend who sincerely believed he'd be a pixie when he died, right?

Emma: I was just going to say that!

Sean: Then I told the crowd, "It doesn't matter what religion you are. Just know that the God of your religion loves you." Now saying something like this might get you elected, but it's silly … and I got my clock cleaned for saying it.

Emma: How? What happened?

Sean: A priest was listening to me, and he asked me a question in front of everyone there.

He asked, "Sean, how do you know God loves you?" I paused and panicked and reached for the only answer I could think of: "I know He loves me because I can feel Him in my heart." I gave the answer my grandmother used to give to me! He jumped all over me and said, "'Feelings' is how you determine if someone loves you?" I once again affirmed that. Now Emma, I will save you thousands of dollars in therapist fees if you will listen closely here.

Emma: You have my undivided attention.

Sean: He then asked me, "Sean, have you ever loved someone, and they said they loved you back—and you felt it in your heart—but the entire time they were cheating on you?" It had just happened to me, so I honestly told him, "Yes." He then said, "So, Sean, you felt loved by that person, but were you really loved?" I answered, "No, I wasn't loved by that person." He continued, "So you felt loved, but you were not, so what were your feelings actually doing?" I answered, "Deceiving me." "Exactly!" he responded. Then he made me use reason. He said, "So you felt loved, but were not, and yet you just told me you know God loves you because you can 'feel it,' when in actuality He may be …" I looked at him and answered, "He may be deceiving me." I was crushed.

Everyone was watching me. There was no way out of this one. The only thing I could do was go on the offensive, so I said to him, "Well how do you know your God loves *you*?"

Emma: What did he say?

Sean: He said, "I'm glad you asked that question because my faith is the only faith that can truly show that God loves us and how deeply He does." It was a bold statement, and some people started calling him "intolerant" and other names.

Emma: Because they could not answer him. Diversion!

Sean: Yep. I, on the other hand, told him to prove his statement because I really wanted to know. He looked at me and outstretched his hands like a cross and said, "Jesus loves us all, brother. He loves every Jew, Christian, Muslim, Hindu, Buddhist, atheist, etc. And He proved it by dying on a cross for our sins."

He just kept holding his arms out like a cross, and the truth hit me like a ton of bricks. Emma, do you want to know how you can tell if someone really loves you? See how much they are willing to sacrifice for you. That's how you know. Let me prove my point. If someone says they love you, does that definitely mean they do?

Emma: Absolutely not. Been there many times.

Sean: Okay, but if they say they love you and then buy you a gift, then you know they love you. Right?

Emma: No! Not at all. In fact, the gift can be a diversion.

Sean: Okay, then how about this. Imagine you are at the mall with your fiancé.

Emma: Is he hot?

Sean: Come on, man! Trying to prove a point here!

Emma: Okay. I am at the mall with my fiancé.

Sean: A man comes up to you with a gun, points it at your head, and says, "I've always hated you, and tonight I'm going to blow your head off!" Your fiancé grabs the gun and points it away from you and toward himself. He says to the man, "Shoot me instead. I trade my life for hers, but promise me after you kill me you will let her go." The gunman promises, shoots your fiancé, and lets you go. Tell me, Emma. Did your fiancé love you?

Emma: Oh my gosh, yes. I'm so sad, and the story isn't even true.

Sean: Yes it is, Emma. It's a true story.

Emma: What are you talking about?

Sean: You already have someone who loves you so much that He laid down His life for you. His name is Jesus. Jesus even says it Himself, "No one has greater love than this, to lay down one's life for one's friends" (John 15:13).

Emma: Wow ... I never really thought of it that way.

Sean: Too many people have forgotten about the cross and what it means. Often, I find Christians thinking that Jesus only died for the people

2,000 years ago, when in reality He died for everyone for all time. When Jesus was on the cross, He saw your face and mine and the sins we would commit, and He willingly died for them. Don't think that God was not in control, even though He was bound by the guards. Jesus said, "No one takes it from me, but I lay it down on my own. I have power to lay it down and power to take it up again. This command I have received from my Father" (John 10:18). He also said, "Do you think that I cannot call upon my Father, and He will not provide me at this moment with more than twelve legions of angels?" (Matthew 26:53). Jesus' death opened up heaven for all. It redeemed mankind so that our sins can be forgiven.

Emma: So we all are saved and go to heaven?

Sean: No, that does not mean everyone goes to heaven. Remember that God has redeemed mankind, but we have to respond to that love. It's our choice. Some reject the gift.

Emma: So if it's our choice, then actually God doesn't shove us into hell.

Sean: Scripture is clear that God desires all mankind to be saved and to come to the knowledge of the truth (1 Timothy 2:4). He does not wish any to perish but all to reach repentance (2 Peter 3:9). But God won't coerce someone to love Him. If someone chooses not to be with God, He can't force them to be with Him, so He gives them what they desire: life without God.

Listen to this excellent quote from C.S. Lewis: "There are only two kinds of people in the end: those who say to God, 'Thy will be done,' and those to whom God says in the end, 'Thy will be done.' All that are in hell chose it. Without that self-choice, there could be no hell. No soul that seriously and constantly desires joy will ever miss it. Those who seek find. To those who knock, it is opened."

You see, Emma, hell is locked from the inside.

Emma: I understand. It's pretty scary that we have free will. I don't want to choose poorly.

Sean: There are a couple of things to remember. First, free will is essential if we are going to love. Love has to be freely given, and God IS love, so there is no way He would make us programmed robots that must do His will like slaves. Second, guess what? You ARE going to choose poorly sometimes, and my guess would be that you have already.

Emma: That's true.

Sean: Don't think you're alone. We all have sinned. But the cross means we're forgiven, and we just have to ask for that forgiveness, confess our sins, and repent. We have a Savior who died on a cross and bore our sins. He who was without sin became sin. Listen to what St. John Paul II wrote about this: "Although Christ, the Holy One, was absolutely sinless, He agreed to take our sins upon Himself. He agreed in order to redeem us; He agreed to bear our sins to fulfill the mission He had received from the Father, who—as the Evangelist John writes—'so loved the world that he gave His only Son, that whoever believes in Him ... may have eternal life' (John 3:16)."

Emma: So God will forgive all of my sins?

Sean: Yes.

Emma: Come on! Even if I kill someone, God will forgive that?

Sean: Yes. If you are truly sorry, God will forgive you. There is only one thing God can't forgive.

Emma: What?

Sean: Someone who does not ask for forgiveness. We must truly be sorry and confess our sins.

One of the reasons I left Buddha was because he did not die for me and save me. He did not open up the gates of heaven for all mankind. Jesus alone did that. I know of no one who, knowing the sins of my heart, would so readily die for me like He did. Think about it. God knows every evil thought and sin you have ever committed and will ever commit—and He still thought you were worth dying for.

Emma: That's hard for me to grasp because there are times when I can't even forgive myself or even look in a mirror.

Sean: Let me read you a story from Scripture. Make sure you listen well …

"Now a leper came to Him, imploring Him, kneeling down to Him and saying to Him, 'If You are willing, You can make me clean.' Then Jesus, moved with compassion, stretched out His hand and touched him, and said to him, 'I am willing; be cleansed.' As soon as He had spoken, immediately the leprosy left him, and he was cleansed."

Emma: Okay, that's cool. He healed the guy. What does that have to do with my not wanting to look at myself in the mirror because of my shame?

Sean: There is way more to this story than Jesus just healing this man. In society back then, if you had leprosy, you became an outcast. You literally had to carry a bell and ring it while shouting, "Unclean!" if people came near you. You would have lived outside the town or city and begged for food. If someone touched you, they would then be "unclean," as well.

Emma: Wow that's depressing. I can't imagine that. What if the guy had a family? None of his children or his wife could ever touch him again, and he would have to just watch them from afar.

Sean: That's right, no one could touch him. But read the Scripture again. What did Jesus do?

Emma: He touched him when He healed him … oh, man. That is beautiful.

Sean: It is. If Jesus touched him, people would have declared that He was unclean, as well, but Jesus knew this man had not been touched by anyone for a long time. He knew this man's loneliness and feelings of rejection. Now Jesus had healed other people from a distance without even seeing them, but this man He touched. Do you think this man, whose skin was falling off of him, wanted to look in a mirror?

Emma: No, he would have been ashamed to look at himself.

Sean: Exactly, so what is God trying to tell you about this encounter from many years ago?

Emma: That even if I can't look at myself, God will look at me because He does not want me feeling lonely or hating myself.

Sean: That's exactly right, Emma. Even if the whole world—including yourself—turns its back on you, God says, "…I will never leave thee nor forsake thee" (Hebrews 13:5).

Emma: It's so hard to comprehend that the Creator of the world even knows me, let alone loves me.

Sean: Yes, it's beyond our comprehension, but it's awesome. He knows us and loves us completely. He says, "…even the hairs of your head have all been counted" (Luke 12:7).

Emma: Okay, so I can see how Jesus got your attention. He has gotten mine. Tell me more. Was there more that made you leave Buddha? I know you revealed some illogical beliefs in Buddhism, like all of us owing an eternal debt, but there being no one to collect it. For me, I mean honestly, just the cross alone is enough for me. When I look at a crucifix, it will actually mean something to me now.

Sean: Remember also that Jesus did not look like the body on your crucifix. It was much worse.

Emma: How much worse?

Sean: Scripture says He was beaten brutally. With spikes in His hands and feet fastening Him to a cross, He slowly suffocated in His own bodily fluids, while His lungs filled up with water. The cross is the greatest sign of love, but I also came to realize something else. This suffering and death opened up the gates of heaven for all people who say "Yes" to His love.

Emma: We talked about this earlier—how there can be meaning in suffering. How just because we can't see anything good coming out of suffering doesn't mean there isn't—just like the death of God on a cross.

Sean: Yes. We always have to look at the cross with both sadness and joy. Sadness that our sins cost so much … and joy that Jesus rose again and conquered death. By His life, death, and resurrection, He proved He IS God. So guess what?

Emma: What?

Scan: If Jesus is God, then Buddha isn't.

Emma: Oh … right.

Sean: Emma, I want to talk to you like a child, not because you are one, but because it's going to be a great way to teach you something powerful that you will remember and be able to share with others. All I need you to do is answer my questions, okay? My intellect compelled me to become Catholic, and my heart was moved by the person of Jesus. I see your heart is being touched by Him, as well, but I want to go back to the intellect again.

Emma: *Fides et ratio*, faith and reason, right? Fire away.

Sean: If God is perfection, can He make a mistake about truth?

Emma: Of course not. Perfection means no error.

Sean: Good. Now Jesus is who?

Emma: God.

Sean: So can Jesus lie and teach error?

Emma: No.

Sean: Right. He can't teach error or sin because He is God in the flesh. Now who knows more about God, God or me?

Emma: Obviously, God.

Sean: Jesus is who?

Emma: God.

Sean: So who knows more about God, Jesus or me?

Emma: Jesus, because He is God and you are not.

Sean: Okay, now was Buddha God?

Emma: No.

Sean: That's right, Buddha said there was no God. So since he was just a man, could he have made a mistake? Could he have been wrong?

Emma: Yes, human beings tend to mess up from time to time.

Sean: So who knows more about God, Buddha or God?

Emma: God.

Sean: Jesus is who?

Emma: God.

Sean: So who knows more about God, Jesus or Buddha?

Emma: Jesus, because He is God.

Sean: Was Muhammad God?

Emma: No, he was a man.

Sean: So could he have been wrong?

Emma: Of course.

Sean: Then who knows more about God, God or Muhammad?

Emma: God.

Sean: Jesus is who?

Emma: God.

Sean: So who knows more about God, Jesus or Muhammad?

Emma: Jesus, because He is God.

Sean: So if Jesus gives us a teaching and Buddha contradicts it and Muhammad contradicts it … who is right in this argument?

Emma: Jesus, because He is God. Whoa … That is so counter-cultural, but it is logically sound.

Sean: Jesus says we die and are judged and go to heaven or hell. Buddha says reincarnation. Who is right?

Emma: It has to be Jesus. He is God.

Sean: That's right. Buddha is wrong. Do you really see this?

Emma: I really do. God would not teach in opposition to Himself, so He would not inspire Buddha to teach in opposition to Jesus.

Sean: Now Buddha said both some good things and some things that are out there. But after he taught, he died. Then he did something very interesting. Do you know what it was?

Emma: No idea.

Sean: He stayed dead.

Emma: That is harsh!

Sean: Follow along, Emma. Now, Muhammad said both some good things and some things that actually scare me. Then he died. Do you know what he did after he died?

Emma: He stayed dead.

Sean: Exactly. Now Jesus said, "Love your enemies and pray for those who persecute you." Then he died. He did something much different than the other two. Do you know what it is?

Emma: He came back to life.

Sean: That's right. He got up! The dead man was resurrected! He also healed the sick, raised people from the dead, and performed many miracles. Neither Muhammad nor Buddha did that. Now when someone heals the sick, walks on water, predicts his own death and resurrection, and then dies and comes back to life … that gets my attention. You know you are going to die one day, right?

Emma: I do.

Sean: If, after death, there actually is a life where there is no more suffering, would you want to be there?

Emma: Of course! If I die, I want to rise again. No doubt about it.

Sean: Then follow the One who did it. Follow the God-man who is alive—not the philosophies and teachings of the dead.

Emma: This is all blowing me away. We have come so far from the woman you spoke of earlier, who said that all religions are the same and worship the same God. Her statement in the light of reason seems so limited and weak—and really insulting to God.

Sean: You are absolutely correct. Jesus went to a lot of trouble to come into the hearts of people by dying on a cross for our sins. For someone to say that the crucifixion of God for the sins of mankind is equal to the philosophy of a human who told us there is no God is an insult to God and our intellect. Now I'm not saying the Buddhists, Muslims, or Hindus are terrible people. I'm just comparing Buddha, Muhammad, and Hindu teaching to Jesus—and they all fail in comparison.

Emma: Well, of course! You are comparing people to God!

Sean: Exactly right. And I think if I share with you a difficult conversation I had to have with a mother and father who lost their child to cancer, you will really be able to see the differences I have been talking about.

The husband came up to me with tears in his eyes and said, "My little girl is dead. Can you help me?"

Emma: Oh my gosh. What did you say?

Sean: First, let me tell you what I would have had to say to him if I were a Buddhist, Hindu, or Muslim. Really listen to hear the differences.

As a Buddhist, I would have had to tell him, "Sir, the reason you are suffering is because you are still holding onto your daughter. The key to happiness is to detach from all want, need, love, and personality. You see, sir, your daughter never really existed. She is an illusion, just as you are. Once you let go and detach from everything, including yourself, you will finally be annihilated and you will be no more. I hope that gives you peace."

Emma: Whoa, okay that would not give me peace. What about a Hindu?

Sean: As a Hindu, I would have to say, "Sir please stop grieving. Your daughter is God, and so are you. We all are, but you don't yet realize it.

She will reincarnate as possibly a worm, rat, frog, mosquito, or kangaroo—depending on what lesson she needs to learn the next time around. But remember that "she" is gone for good. Her energy moves onto the next level until finally all that was left of your daughter is annihilated and her energy becomes one with the energy of Hitler and Stalin—because they were God, too. Also, if your daughter suffered, that is a good thing because that was something she had to learn in this life to help in her next life. I hope this brings you peace."

Emma: God has amnesia? We are God, but we don't know it? This is crazy. Okay, what does the Muslim say?

Sean: "I am so sorry for your loss. I pray Allah will be merciful. Her chances of Paradise are not very good if she was not a Muslim, and also the great prophet has revealed that hell is filled with more women than men."

Emma: Another disaster. Well, what did you actually say, as a Christian?

Sean: When he asked me, "Can you help me?" I told him I could not, but that there was someone who could. I told him that God loves him so much that He died on a cross to open up the gates of heaven for us all. I told him that our God is not a God of the dead but of the living. That if he would just hold onto Jesus I knew that when he died, Our Lord, who rose from the dead, will also raise him and bring him into His arms where He will "wipe away every tear." I then told him I could imagine that Jesus would turn his shoulder and from behind Jesus his little girl would run into his arms. Jesus would say, "I told you I had her. I love her even more than you do."

Emma: Now, that would comfort me.

Sean: Emma, God does not want you annihilated! He does not want you wandering through space and coming back as an animal to make amends for your mistakes. He wants to lift those burdens from you and forgive you. Jesus has come to set us free! Buddha says we owe an eternal debt. That burden is unbearable. Jesus came to pay that debt for us by dying on a cross for our sins so we can cast our burdens on Him and receive

His forgiveness! The core teachings of Buddhism and Christianity are in complete opposition to each other. One says, annihilate yourselves by getting rid of who you are. Jesus says, "For God so loved the world He gave His only begotten Son so that whoever believes in Him shall not parish but have everlasting life."

Emma: I have never really understood until now just how different Jesus and Buddha are.

Sean: Let me show you the contrast even more. Peter Kreeft explains, "A Christian acts with free willed agape, which is an active love, and Buddhism teaches an impersonal, universal feeling of compassion." He continues, "Karma and agape lead the disciple to do similar strikingly selfless deeds but in strikingly different spirits." He tells the Buddhist story of a man who gives his cloak to a beggar who was in fact a robber. The Buddhist explanation for this deed was not, "because I loved him" but rather, "It was the enlightened thing to do, for if you were freezing and had two gloves on one hand and none on the other hand, would it not be the enlightened thing to do to give one of the gloves to the bare hand?" Kreeft continues, "The point of charity for a Buddhist is not the welfare of the recipient but the liberation of the giver from the burden of self."

Emma: Wow, I see the difference. One is coming from a true altruistic place, while the other is really only working on himself. It's all about his liberation instead of a deep love that expects nothing in return and is given with no other motive than, "I love you because Jesus loved me first."

Sean: You are definitely grasping this, but are you aware that Jesus also built something? Do you know what it is?

Emma: I'm not sure.

Sean: A church. The Catholic Church. Listen to this Scripture: "And so I say to you, you are Peter, and upon this rock **I will build my church**, and the gates of the netherworld shall not prevail against it" (Matthew 16:18).

Emma: Well, that is clear as day. God clearly says He is building a church, but why do you say it was the Catholic Church?

Sean: Because there was only one church for over 1,000 years. Guess which one?

Emma: The Catholic Church.

Sean: So guess which church is His?

Emma: The Catholic Church.

Sean: Now Emma, if God built the world a Church, do you think He wants you to be in it?

Emma: I would hope so.

Sean: Yes, He wants everyone in it. It does matter what religion we are, or Jesus wouldn't have built a Church.

Emma: Does that mean everyone else is going to hell?

Sean: Ha, you sound like my old Baptist minister!

Emma: But if we are not in Jesus' Church, how can anyone else get to heaven?

Sean: Here is what the Church teaches: God wills that all people be saved. Now there are some people who have never heard of Jesus. So does that mean "tough luck" for them, and they go to hell? What about a person who is severely handicapped and has a very limited capacity to think? Would they go to hell, as well? Let me give you an example. If there were a man way off in a foreign land with very few people and the name Jesus had never reached his ears, yet he looked at the world and knew there must be God and was a man who cared for the poor and lonely, we as Catholics believe there is hope for this man. It is quite possible that when he dies he will meet Jesus and say, "Oh my Lord, I have always loved you, but now I know your name!"

Emma: Wow, that's amazing.

Sean: Yes, God's mercy is infinite. You must not think of God as someone who is in charge of a vault trying to keep people out. He is a loving father trying to bring his children home for the great banquet! His mercy reaches out in ways we can't comprehend. When the poor man who had never heard of Jesus was helping the poor, do you know who he was encountering and helping?

Emma: Who?

Sean: Jesus. Listen to Jesus in this Scripture passage: "Then the King will say to those on his right, 'Come, you who are blessed by my Father; take your inheritance, the kingdom prepared for you since the creation of the world. For I was hungry and you gave me something to eat, I was thirsty and you gave me something to drink, I was a stranger and you invited me in, I needed clothes and you clothed me, I was sick and you looked after me, I was in prison and you came to visit me.'

"Then the righteous will answer him, 'Lord, when did we see you hungry and feed you, or thirsty and give you something to drink? When did we see you a stranger and invite you in, or needing clothes and clothe you? When did we see you sick or in prison and go to visit you?'

"The King will reply, 'Truly I tell you, whatever you did for one of the least of these brothers and sisters of mine, you did for me.'"

Emma: That is beautiful.

Sean: It is, but we must have balance, as well. You and I have little excuse. If you sit on a couch all day playing video games and claim you were ignorant of Jesus, I'm sorry but that is not going to be a good excuse. The poor man who helped the sick and lonely was ignorant (not by his own fault) of Jesus, so that ignorance helps lessen his accountability.

Here is a quote from the Catechism: "This affirmation is not aimed at those who, through no fault of their own, do not know Christ and his Church: Those who, through no fault of their own, do not know the Gospel of Christ or his Church, but who nevertheless seek God with a sincere heart, and, moved by grace, try in their actions to do his will as they know it through the dictates of their conscience—those too may achieve eternal salvation.

"Although in ways known to himself God can lead those who, through no fault of their own, are ignorant of the Gospel, to that faith without which it is impossible to please him, the Church still has the obligation and also the sacred right to evangelize all men" (CCC 847-848).

Emma: That is so deep. Seriously, I have learned so many incorrect things about the Church. It doesn't want to condemn ... it wants to help!

Sean: You have no idea how much I wish the rest of the world could hear what you are saying and growing to know. Unfortunately, they don't take the time to read what the Church teaches and instead listen to Bill Maher and other anti-religious people who are clueless about what the Church really teaches and why.

Chapter 8

The Resurrection: What It Is, What It Isn't, and Why It Matters

Emma: Okay, so I believe that if Jesus really performed miracles and rose from the dead that He is God—case closed. But how do we know this actually happened? How can we know that Jesus really rose from the dead?

Sean: Very good, Emma. We have to take a look at this because all of Christianity rests on whether or not Jesus resurrected. We're going to dig in here. Some of this may get a bit tedious, but I'll do my best to keep it as short as possible. If at the end of this you want to read more, there are two people you MUST read. The first is N.T. Wright. Read or listen to anything of his on the resurrection. I have read his 800-page masterpiece, *The Resurrection of the Son of God*, three times. It's amazing. I also beg you to read anything by William Lane Craig and watch his debates on YouTube. His website is ReasonableFaith.org. These two men have, with charity, destroyed any contenders who try to disprove the resurrection, and Craig has KO'd all opponents debating the existence of God.

Emma: I'll give them a try, once you finish and let me see that there is reason to dig in deeper.

Sean: Excellent, that's all I can ask. In this short time, I am afraid I will not do it justice, so promise you will read those authors I told you about.

Emma: Okay, I promise. This really matters to me. My life—and, if there is a God, my soul—depends on it. So prove to me that Jesus rose from the dead.

Sean: I can't prove that, Emma. But here is what I'm saying. There is the claim that Jesus rose (resurrected) supernaturally from the dead, but there are people postulating theories that do not rely on the supernatural to explain this event. For example, some people have said that someone stole the body of Jesus. What we are going to do is become detectives and look at all the theories to see which one makes the most sense.

Now the reason there is any question at all is because there are some in the world who do not believe in God and therefore do not believe in miracles. If miracles are a possibility, then it's not impossible for Jesus to rise from the dead. If someone does not believe in God, then of course there are no such things as miracles, so they are going to come up with other theories within the scope of naturalism (meaning natural explanations instead of supernatural ones). We should always first seek a natural explanation with any miraculous claim, but if the natural does not work, then we need to look outside the natural world at the possibility of the supernatural.

Emma: It seems odd to me that someone would already dismiss the miraculous as a possibility if they are trying to be scientific. It sounds like they have an agenda and will only work to prove their agenda.

Sean: You're right, Emma. If we are going to be truly scientific in our approach, we need to be open to the evidence and let that lead us to our conclusions—not the other way around.

Emma: I have to ask you this question: If it was proven beyond the shadow of a doubt that Jesus' body was found and He was not resurrected, would you still worship Him?

Sean: Absolutely not! Even St. Paul speaks about this: "And if Christ has not been raised, then empty too is our preaching; empty, too, is your faith" (1 Corinthians 15:14).

Emma: I like that. You are serious about this. You're not just believing in fairy tales and pixies to make you feel better.

Sean: I think you know me better than that by now. Both my heart and my intellect compel me to faith in Jesus. After all the research I've done, I'm convinced that the supernatural resurrection of Jesus is the best explanation for the faith of the early Church—and no other theories can explain why Christianity is here today.

Let's first talk about what resurrection is and what it isn't. Many people today incorrectly think that resurrection is when you die and your soul goes to heaven. That is not resurrection. Resurrection is a two-staged event. When you die, your soul (if you are in a state of grace, of course) goes to heaven, and your body goes into the ground or is cremated. The next stage happens when Jesus returns at the end of time and our bodies are resurrected. They are transformed into supernatural bodies like Jesus' and rejoin our souls. The souls that are in heaven now are not complete because they do not have their bodies.

Emma: Wow, okay, I never knew that.

Sean: Yes, N.T. Wright refers to this as "life after ... life after death." And speaking of N.T. Wright, I am going to briefly use his work to explain why the resurrection is the best explanation of the Christian faith. He speaks about mutations that took place within Christianity that can only be explained by the resurrection.

Emma: I'm ready, but very skeptical.

Sean: Let's talk about what the ancient world believed about death. Some skeptics claim that 2,000 years ago people believed in all kinds of oddities like resurrection because scientific advancements had yet to teach them that dead people stay dead. This is actually ludicrous. In ancient paganism, there were many different theories about death, but no one believed in resurrection. The massive evidence confirms that people of the ancient world knew that dead people stayed dead. Again, no one in ancient paganism believed in resurrection.

Emma: Okay, I get the point. You are really emphasizing it. Why?

Sean: Be patient. I'll explain soon.

Now ancient Judaism believed that God was the creator, and one day He would set the world in order again and bring justice. Judaism had a spectrum of belief in the afterlife. Some Jews believed that at the end of time everyone all together would be resurrected from the dead, but it was not really clear what that would look like. There is a brief reference in the book of Daniel that mentions resurrected bodies being like a "shining star," but that's about it. The Sadducees (a sect of Judaism) did not believe in resurrection or any afterlife. Resurrection in Judaism was more of a side note. It wasn't a major doctrine of Judaism.

Emma: Okay, following along here. The Jews held different beliefs about resurrection, and it wasn't a main focus.

Sean: Good, keep following along. I know this may seem tedious, but if you really want evidence, you have to really follow this. Take your time, and I know you will get it.

Now, history reveals that the hope of life after death in Christianity came from the Jews and not the pagan world. N.T. Wright demonstrates that, while the reality of resurrection came to Christianity from Judaism, it was drastically transformed. I quote him: "This Jewish hope has undergone remarkable modifications or mutations within early Christianity, which can be plotted consistently right across the first two centuries. And these mutations are so striking, in an area of human experience where societies tend to be very conservative, that they force the historian, not least the would-be scientific historian, to ask, 'Why did they occur?'"

Emma: So Wright is saying that the Christians' belief about resurrection changed so drastically that there needs to be an amazing explanation as to why that would happen.

Sean: Exactly!

Emma: And he is going to say it is the resurrection of Jesus, right?

Sean: Correct—and you will see why.

Emma: Okay, I'm still following. Keep going.

Sean: Let's go through the mutations Wright presents. I want you to know while I do this that I will be using Scripture as historical text and not as the inspired Word of God. I do believe they are inspired, but for our case I want to just use them as historical documents because they are top-notch historical accounts.

Emma: Good. If you just say the Bible is the Word of God, I am not going to believe you, so you need another path to my brain.

Sean: You got it. So the first mutation is that there is virtually no spectrum of belief about resurrection within early Christianity. Remember that the Christians came from many differing sects of Judaism, so one would think that they would have varying opinions about resurrection, like in Judaism. But this is not the case.

Emma: So we don't see any Christians believing like the Sadducees that there is no resurrection.

Sean: Correct.

Emma: Do any of them believe that they will be shining like a star, as in the book of Daniel you told me about?

Sean: No, but great point! I will get to that in a bit. There is virtually no spectrum of belief about resurrection. It is nailed down tight.

The second mutation is that in Judaism, resurrection is important, but not really important. Then in Christianity, all of a sudden resurrection is the center of everything. When talking about how much ink was given to the resurrection in Christianity, Wright says, "Take away the resurrection and you lose the entire New Testament, and most of the Church fathers, as well."

Emma: Okay, that's easy to follow. All of a sudden, resurrection is a really big deal. It is *the* deal.

Sean: Right.

Emma: By the way, you mentioned the Church fathers. Who are they?

Sean: They are the ones that the disciples taught and passed the faith onto.

Emma: We have their writings? Seriously? These guys who learned the faith right from the apostles wrote things down?

Sean: Yes! I know that sounds exciting—and it is—but let's not get off track here. Let's stay with the mutations.

Emma: Right.

Sean: The third mutation has to do with what resurrection truly is. There was ambiguity as to what kind of body you would have when resurrected. Some Jews saw it as just your original body, and, as I said before, some said it would be like a shining star. However, from the beginning, the Christian belief was that we would receive our body back, but it would be transformed. The resurrected body would be supernatural. It would be incorruptible and would not decay or die, as St. Paul says in 1 Corinthians.

Emma: So all of a sudden the Christians have resurrection finely tuned instead having a spectrum of beliefs about it.

Sean: Correct. Now the fourth mutation in the early Christian belief of resurrection is that "the resurrection," was now a two-stage event. Remember I told you that the Jews who did believe in resurrection believed it would be one event at the end of time. The resurrection of Jesus would be such a foreign concept because to them the resurrection would happen to everyone at the same time.

Emma: That's weird. This is *all* weird. Why did they start believing all of these things that were outside of their belief system?

Sean: I love the way you phrased that! They *are* believing things that would not even register on their radar ... all of a sudden. Hmm. What must have happened? Now let me finish with the rest of the mutations Wright talks about. Then we'll dive into the "why" of it.

There are other mutations, but for the sake of time I will only share one more; and this is really important to understand. Nobody in Judaism was expecting a Messiah who was going to die, so of course no one would have imagined him rising from the dead. Yet an amazing mutation takes place. Remember that the Jews were expecting the Messiah to be a warrior who would come in battle and free the Jews by destroying the pagans. He would rebuild or cleanse the temple and bring the peace of God to the entire world. In their eyes, it would seem that Jesus did none of those things. No Jew would have thought that the dead corpse hanging on the cross was God's anointed Messiah! Yet from the very beginning, Christians affirmed that Jesus was the Messiah, precisely because of the resurrection.

Emma: This is a big deal. If they are expecting a warrior who would fight in battle and win freedom—and instead their guy is dead on a cross—I can see how they would have thought, "Wow, we picked a loser. We were way off with this guy." Yet instead, they think the opposite. Very strange indeed!

Sean: Precisely! Think about it. There is no way that the Christian faith in Jesus as Messiah could have originated unless Jesus resurrected! History reveals that there were other messianic Jewish movements before and after the life of Jesus. Those movements always ended with the death of that leader. The followers who escaped the fate of the leader had to make a decision: either give up the fight or find a new Messiah. The Christians could have just grabbed one of the apostles to carry the torch as their new Messiah—but they didn't.

Now some scholars have tried to say that the disciples felt that even though Jesus was crucified, His message burned on in the hearts of the disciples.

Therefore, they thought he was the Messiah, and they carried on the mission.

Some skeptics also say that the apostles were so grief-stricken that they had a vision or hallucination of Jesus, but this is simply implausible. Let's learn from history. In AD 70, Simon bar Giora led a messianic movement, and, like all the other messianic leaders, he was flogged and executed. N.T. Wright does a superb job with this in his paper, "Can Science Believe in the Resurrection," explaining what would have gone on in the hearts of his followers after Simon bar Giora was killed: "Suppose we go to Rome in AD 70 and there witness the flogging and execution of Simon bar Giora, the supposed king of the Jews, brought back in Titus' triumph. Suppose we imagine a few Jewish revolutionaries, three days or three weeks later ...

The first one says, 'You know, I think Simon really was the Messiah—and he still is!'

The others would be puzzled. Of course he isn't; the Romans got him, as they always do. If you want a Messiah, you'd better find another one.

'Ah,' says the first, 'but I believe he's been raised from the dead.'

'What do you mean?' his friends ask. 'He's dead and buried.'

'Oh no,' replies the first, 'I believe he's been exalted to heaven.'

The others look puzzled. All the righteous martyrs are with God, everybody knows that; their souls are in God's hands; that doesn't mean they've already been raised from the dead. Anyway, the resurrection will happen to us all at the end of time, not to one person in the middle of continuing history.

'No,' replies the first, 'you don't understand. I've had a strong sense of God's love surrounding me. I have felt God forgiving me—forgiving us all. I've had my heart strangely warmed. What's more, last night, I saw Simon; he was there with me ...'

The others interrupt, now angry. We can all have visions. Plenty of people dream about recently dead friends. Sometimes it's very vivid. That doesn't mean they've been raised from the dead. It certainly doesn't mean that one of them is the Messiah. And if your heart has been warmed, then sing a psalm; don't make wild claims about Simon."

Emma: That is actually kinda funny. What you are saying is that it is impossible to claim that the Christians' early belief in the resurrection came about by the disciples' having a vision or hallucination of Jesus or by feeling their hearts burning with his mission. First of all, if the apostles just had visions of Jesus, they would not have said He was resurrected. They would have said He was dead. Okay, I truly get this. Visions do not lead one to believe in resurrection.

Sean: Before you make your next point, let me show you a really cool story in Scripture that shows us precisely that visions don't make people believe someone is raised from the dead. This is the story from the Acts of the Apostles, where Peter was arrested and put in jail and freed by an angel: "Then the angel said to him, 'Put on your clothes and sandals.' And Peter did so. 'Wrap your cloak around you and follow me,' the angel told him. Peter followed him out of the prison, but he had no idea that what the angel was doing was really happening; he thought he was seeing a vision. They passed the first and second guards and came to the iron gate leading to the city. It opened for them by itself, and they went through it. When they had walked the length of one street, suddenly the angel left him.

Then Peter came to himself and said, 'Now I know without a doubt that the Lord has sent his angel and rescued me from Herod's clutches and from everything the Jewish people were hoping would happen.'

When this had dawned on him, he went to the house of Mary the mother of John, also called Mark, where many people had gathered and were praying. Peter knocked at the outer entrance, and a servant named Rhoda came to answer the door. When she recognized Peter's voice, she was so overjoyed she ran back without opening it and exclaimed, 'Peter is at the door!'

'You're out of your mind,' they told her. When she kept insisting that it was so, they said, '**It must be his angel.**'

But Peter kept on knocking, and when they opened the door and saw him, they were astonished. Peter motioned with his hand for them to be quiet and described how the Lord had brought him out of prison. 'Tell James and the other brothers and sisters about this,' he said, and then he left for another place."

Emma: That is cool! She tells them that Peter is at the door, and they think it just means that Peter is dead! This is exciting! If the apostles saw only visions of Jesus, they would have had the same reaction as when they heard that Peter was at the door. They would have just thought, "Oh well, his ghost came to us, so that means He is dead and with God." They never would have said, "Wow that means He is resurrected and God the Messiah!".

Sean: Right, so go on with your second point.

Emma: They also would never have believed He was the Messiah after seeing visions or having their hearts warmed by his mission because if your Messiah was crucified, that means he was NOT the Messiah. Instead, they must have been dejected and embarrassed.

Sean: They *were* dejected. They ran away and hid.

Emma: So, some claim that visions and heart warmings could have brought about the belief in the resurrection of Jesus, but we have just proven from history that that is impossible. I'm sure the followers of the other men who claimed to be the Messiah believed in their guy, too, but we don't see anyone claiming that their professed Messiah had risen from the dead after he was killed. They just went home.

Sean: So we need to ask, "What is the best answer to account for all of these mutations?"

Emma: Well, what are some other things that people say to explain away the resurrection? What other theories are there?

Sean: Let's go through the most prominent theories, though few historians give them much credit, and most believe that those who try to advance these theories are really grasping at straws.

1. <u>Hallucination and Visions</u> — We have already gone over this one. We've shown that a vision doesn't mean someone is resurrected. It means he is dead. Remember that the disciples emphatically did not say it was visions. And they walked with Jesus, touched Him, and ate with Him! Also, it has been shown time and again that groups of people do not have giant hallucinations together.

2. <u>Wrong Tomb</u> — The women went to the wrong tomb and therefore thought the tomb was empty when, in fact, it was not. This one is ridiculous. Scripture tells us that Joseph of Arimathea brought Jesus to his own tomb for burial, so everyone knew where it was. Besides, even if they did forget where Jesus was buried, eventually the Pharisees and Romans would have discovered his body and dragged it out for all to see to put an end to the claims of resurrection.

3. <u>The Swoon Theory</u> — Jesus was not really dead on the cross, but survived the execution, crawled out of the tomb—and the disciples healed Him. This is my favorite one to laugh at. First of all, the Romans knew how to kill and kill well. Scripture is clear that Jesus was already dead before He was taken off the cross. Anyone who ever tells you that Jesus was not taken off the cross, but was left there and just rotted off, is doing so with no historical evidence whatsoever. It comes from a bias against the supernatural. Now back to the swoon theory. Can you imagine the disciples' faces when they see a half-dead, bloodied Jesus crawling to them? Would they be thinking, "Wow, Jesus … you are God!"?

Emma: No! Oh man, I'm sorry but that is really funny.

Sean: It is laughable. What they would have said is, "Boy, you are one lucky and tough dude, but you are NOT the Messiah!"

4. Stolen body — This theory states that the disciples or the Pharisees stole the body, and that's why the tomb was empty. Again, this falls short like the others.

Emma: Oh, let me explain this one! This one is easy!

Sean: Okay, go for it, my genius friend.

Emma: First of all, the Pharisees would have no reason to steal the body. And even if they did, they would have produced the corpse to put an end to the resurrection stories being told. In fact, I think they would have enjoyed doing that. Secondly, the apostles would not steal the body because they were not expecting the Messiah to die or rise from the dead, so it would not even be on their radar screen to pull a hoax like that. Lastly, check me on this, Sean, but the apostles were killed for believing Jesus resurrected and was God the Messiah, right?

Sean: They were brutally killed, except for John; he was banished.

Emma: So again, if the apostles saw their Messiah crucified, it would make no sense for them to steal the body and claim resurrection because 1. No one was expecting a dying—let alone rising—Messiah. 2. When your messiah was crucified, it meant you had the wrong guy. They would have been mad at Jesus for tricking them into thinking He was the Messiah when He wasn't. They would not defend the guy but rather distance themselves from Him and be rethinking how gullible they really were. 3. Why in the world would they make up a story that would get them killed for a lie? Do you know what I am trying to say?

Sean: Yes, I do. You are saying that if Jesus did not rise from the dead, then one would have to believe that the apostles stole the body and made up an outrageous story. Can you imagine Peter saying, "Okay guys, listen … they killed Jesus so that means He is not the Messiah and we were wrong. And even though we would never think this, I say we steal His body and tell everyone He is resurrected! Then the Romans will come for us all, including our wives and children, and kill us for spreading a ridiculous lie! Now, who's with me?!" Sounds a bit like a Monty Python skit, doesn't it?

Emma: Totally! No one dies for a lie. We die for what we believe in. The apostles truly believed Jesus really was raised from the dead physically—not like a spirit—and they were willing to die for that belief! Okay, so what else do you have for me?

Sean: 5. The next theory is Legendary Embellishment. This theory claims that over time the Christians came to a belief in resurrection through stories being told over and over again—stories that grew more fanciful as time went by, eventually leading them to claim resurrection. For example, some say that after Jesus died, the apostles said that Jesus' message was still alive in their hearts. Then that phrase went on to be that Jesus lives in their hearts, then turning into, "Jesus is alive," until finally the message became, "Jesus is resurrected."

Emma: There is a problem with that?

Sean: There is a *huge* problem with that. From very early on, the disciples believed in the resurrection. Scripture sources date very early to the event and even earlier to the oral traditions—to within possibly months of the events. It is a documented fact that it takes at least a couple of generations before legendary embellishment can occur. There simply was not enough time for this to happen. Resurrection was believed from the very beginning. Interestingly, the time when legendary embellishment would have arisen was at the time of the writing of the gnostic gospels.

Emma: What are the gnostic gospels?

Sean: These were embellished stories about Jesus that the Church has always known were late writings filled with nonsensical stories, such as a cross speaking.

Emma: So the gnostic gospels that are full of fanciful tales were written right at the time when researchers say legendary embellishment would occur—and yet the canonical resurrection stories in Scripture do not contain any legendary embellishment?

Sean: After the resurrection, the Gospel writers combed through the Old Testament trying to make sense of what just happened, so we see biblical quotation, allusion, and echo, but when you look at the Passion narratives in the Gospels they are left untouched. It is raw. We see very interesting details in them that would not have been "made up."

Emma: Such as?

Sean: It is fascinating that the first witnesses of the resurrection were women. This would have been embarrassing for the disciples because unfortunately a woman's testimony was not worth anything back then. No one would have made that up as part of the story because it adds no validation to the story AND is embarrassing to the disciples! If they were going to make up a resurrection story of Jesus appearing to anybody, it would have been to the men, especially Peter. We can read that by the time Paul starts writing about it, he has already done away with the women as witnesses because that would actually hurt his story when trying to convert people.

Emma: Then why would anyone use women at that time as the primary first witnesses if their witness is not even admissible?

Sean: Bingo. Also, there is something fascinating about how the Gospels speak about Jesus' resurrected body. Go back and read the accounts. They all seem to recognize Him … but He is different. It is Jesus, but He has changed. The resurrection accounts read as if someone were trying to explain something that they just can't explain. Now remember the only reference the disciples would have had about what the resurrected body may look like was from the book of Daniel.

Emma: Oh right, He would be shining like a star.

Sean: But do they portray Him this way?

Emma: No! They are having trouble even putting into words what they're seeing. If they wanted to make up the story, they would have had Him shining like a star.

Sean: So you see here that we sure have a dilemma for the skeptic.

Emma: Yes, there is a huge problem. Not one of their theories explains why the early Christians would believe Jesus was physically raised from the dead.

Sean: Precisely, so after we exhaust all possible natural explanations, we need to look to supernatural explanations. The resurrection explains everything: the mutations, the women as witnesses, why He was not described as shining as a star, lack of legendary embellishment, and their willingness to die for Him.

Emma: I see it. There is no way there would have been a Christian faith if Jesus did not really rise from the dead physically.

Sean: Right. The Scriptures, which are excellent historical documents, reveal that on the third day the tomb was empty and that the disciples ate and drank and walked with Jesus after He died. That is why they said He resurrected.

So, in summary, let me tell you that the majority of New Testament scholars today (not just Christian scholars, but skeptics, as well) affirm that:

1. Jesus was crucified.
2. He was buried by Joseph of Arimathea.
3. On the Sunday morning following the crucifixion, the tomb of Jesus was found empty by a group of his women followers.
4. Numerous times, individuals and groups of people experienced appearances of Jesus alive from the dead. Even one of the most skeptical New Testament scholars of our time, Gert Lüdemann, said, "It may be taken as historically certain that Peter and the disciples had experiences after Jesus' death in which Jesus appeared to them as the risen Christ."

Emma: The skeptics believe that the disciples and others saw Jesus after His death?!

Sean: Yes!

Emma: So if they attest to these facts, why can't they see that the only explanation that would explain the faith of the Christians is the resurrection? I mean, seriously! They believe that Jesus appeared to individuals and groups after His death. Even I understand that it could not have been just visions or hallucinations. It had to be His resurrected body. We have been over this! Why won't they believe what the evidence reveals?

Sean: Remember what I told you: Many of them come into this search biased from the beginning—not believing in God and miracles in the first place.

Emma: But that is just wrong! That is not scientific and not honest.

Sean: Agreed! Emma, in a short amount of time you have grasped a ton of information. Time for your final exam.

Emma: Bring it.

Sean: First question: If there had only been an empty tomb, but no appearances of Jesus, what would you conclude?

Emma: That someone stole the body because that was common back then.

Sean: Yes, and that is what the apostles would have concluded, as well. Scripture even makes reference to that theory. Next question: What if the apostles saw apparitions of Jesus, but the tomb was not empty?

Emma: They would have concluded that Jesus was dead and not alive, but exalted into heaven. They would have thought of Him not as the Messiah, but just as a man that they erroneously put their faith in. Visions were common like they are today, so visions do not lead to resurrection.

Sean: Also know that Jesus had a standard burial. A standard burial was a two-step process. First, the body would be wrapped in linen and laid on a stone table within the tomb, and it would be surrounded with and covered with spices. The reason for the spices was to help with the smell because after the body had been laid on the slab, the family or friends of the dead man would come back in to make sure the body had decomposed. Once it had decomposed, they would then take the bones of the person and put them in an ossuary to be placed on a shelf in the tomb. Often entire families would be buried together, and there they remained shelved together. My point is that if the disciples just had visions, eventually someone was going to collect Jesus' bones in the ossuary and produce them, saying, "Umm, He is not resurrected. I have His bones right here."

Emma: That would be "game over."

Sean: Correct. Okay, next. Now, if we have an empty tomb and appearances after His death, appearances where He eats and drinks and walks with people, what do we have?

Emma: Resurrection. No way around it.

Sean: Great. Now bonus questions. Why does the Vision/Hallucinations theory not work?

Emma: Because visions just meant the person was dead, not alive. Five hundred people witnessed Jesus alive, and they would not all have the same hallucinations. Besides, like you said, they wouldn't hallucinate something that would not even be on their radar. They weren't even expecting a dying OR rising Messiah, and if they were going to hallucinate, Jesus would have been shining like a star because that is the image they were familiar with.

Sean: One more important thing to know: The disciple James did not believe in Jesus at first; he was a skeptic. He was not buying into the program, so he would not have hallucinated visions of Jesus exalted into heaven. Because he did not believe yet, James became a great witness and martyr for the faith. Why would James become a believer after Jesus was crucified? Something amazing must have happened to have a skeptic (who was proven right by the crucifixion) become a martyr for the faith. If he saw Jesus raised from the dead, that would do it. And guess what … Scripture tells us that Jesus appeared to James.

Emma: Well that demolishes the idea that they wanted to believe in Him so badly they hallucinated. James did not *want* to believe in Him!

Sean: Great. Now explain why Legendary Embellishment won't explain the faith of the Christians?

Emma: It takes at least two to three generations for embellishment to occur, and the belief in the resurrection of Jesus happened right away. They don't describe Jesus "shining like a star," which they would have done to make the story "pop!" Also, since He appeared to 500 witnesses, those witnesses could have come and demonstrated that the embellishments were not true.

Sean: Yes, St. Paul is very clear in saying that many of the eyewitnesses of Jesus' resurrection were still alive, so people could go to them to confirm the story. Okay now, how about the Swoon Theory?

Emma: Don't insult me. The Romans knew how to kill people, and Jesus would not have survived. But if by some miracle He did, He would not be an impressive Messiah crawling out of His grave covered in blood, half-alive and begging for medical attention!

Sean: The Wrong Tomb theory?

Emma: Again, this is a joke. History reveals that they knew where Jesus was buried, but even if there were an error, eventually they would have turned up the body and produced it.

Sean: So basically, scholars such as N.T. Wright and William Lane Craig have demolished the other theories. So what are we left with?

Emma: Resurrection. I get it. But I do have one question for you—and it may throw you for a loop.

Sean: Let's hear it. This is why we're here.

Emma: There are inconsistencies in the Bible, even with the resurrection accounts. One Gospel says there was one angel, and the other says there are two angels, etc. How do you justify that? Why such contradictions?

Sean: Great question! In actuality, it is the fact that they are different that compels me to believe that they are authentic. Here is what I mean. I want to give you two examples. The first is from N. T. Wright, who tells of a famous true story of a heated argument that broke out during a seminar containing some of the most brilliant men in the world. One of the men brandished a poker from the fireplace!

Emma: He took a hot poker out of the fire to go at someone?

Sean: And I quote: "When we plunge into the stories of the first Easter Day—the accounts we find in the closing chapters of the four canonical gospels—we find that, notoriously, the accounts do not fit snugly together. How many women went to the tomb, and how many angels or men did they meet there? Did the disciples meet Jesus in Jerusalem or Galilee or both? And so on. At this point I am fond of invoking the splendid story of what happened in October 1946 when Karl Popper gave a paper at Wittgenstein's seminar in King's, as written up in that recent book *Wittgenstein's Poker*. Several highly intelligent men—men who would modestly have agreed that they were among the most intelligent men in the world at the time—were in the room as Wittgenstein brandished a poker about and then left abruptly, but none of them could quite agree afterwards as to what precisely had happened. But, as with Cambridge in 1946, so with Jerusalem in AD 30 (or whenever it was): Surface discrepancies do not mean that nothing happened. Indeed, they are a reasonable indication that something remarkable happened."

I hope that makes sense to you. When something amazing or traumatic is happening usually most of the testimonies will conflict. Again this does not mean something did not happen, but rather that something shocking and amazing did happen. Let me give you another example:

I was teaching my eighth-grade religion class and wanted to cover this exact topic we are speaking about. While I was standing in front of my desk (with all eyes on me) I pretended to pick up a bunch of tacks off my table but then switched them out for folded pieces of paper without anyone seeing me.

I then did some really random things like: Sitting in my chair then standing up fast, sneezing, and tapping my feet. Then I told the class that I wanted to see how many kids I could hit with the tacks (that they still perceived to be in my hand). They thought I was kidding, of course. I then took my hand and threw the paper at them. The class went wild! They ducked, screamed, and freaked out. They thought their religion teacher had just thrown tacks at them. I walked around the room and touched one of them on the head and put a pen in the hand of another student while this commotion was going on. I then instantly told them to write down, with as much detail as possible, everything that had just happened.

Emma: It was all different.

Sean: Yep. Some thought I had touched all of the students' heads. One girl thought I threw paper and tacks. The list goes on and on. In fact, some chose to write about the emotion of the event, while others wrote about the physical events. This helps us to understand the Gospels. You see, each writer is coming from a different place and focusing on different things. Seeing a discrepancy does not mean that nothing happened, it means something amazing *did* happen.

Emma: Thank you! That had me worried, but now I get it.

Sean: I also want to drive another point home about the resurrection. St. Paul was a persecutor and hater of Jesus and His followers. He truly believed that they were doing evil and gave orders to execute Christians. He held a place of authority and held Roman citizenship. Then history records that he became a believer in the resurrection and one of the greatest Christians who ever lived, composing most of the New Testament and eventually being beheaded for his faith. Why would he change his position, lose his stature, and be put to death for someone he had been persecuting? Scripture gives us the answer. Jesus appeared to him and spoke to him.

That is the only logical conclusion we can draw for the epic turnaround in this man.

Emma: He must have had an encounter with Jesus because Paul believed that persecuting the Christians was a good and noble thing.

Sean: Also, not only are the the life of Jesus and account of His crucifixion recorded in all four Gospels, but non-Christian sources report the event, too. Jewish historian Josephus and the Roman historian Tacitus are just two of those sources. Jesus was a real historical person, and His life, death, and resurrection are well-attested.

Emma: I still need to hear and read all about this again, but my mind has totally been schooled. It is logical and reasonable to believe that Jesus rose from the dead. But ...

Chapter 9

The Bible: Is It Reliable?

Sean: Here it comes! I've been waiting for this question.

Emma: Do you really know what I'm going to ask?

Sean: Yes, and I'm surprised it didn't come earlier.

Emma: Okay, well why should we trust the Bible anyway? I mean, we are talking about the crucifixion, but that was written down almost 2,000 years ago? How can we trust such an old document?

Sean: I'm proud of you for realizing the importance of this question. Let's set the record straight about this whole "How can we trust such ancient documents?" thing. I hear this a lot, so I'm glad we can talk about it to clear the air. Remember this: It is not how old the document is overall that should raise concern of a letter of antiquity, but rather the time span between the actual event and when it was recorded.

Think about this: Imagine that your great, great, great, great grandfather did something amazing, and it was recorded. Which scenario would you trust more?: 1. He did something amazing and his son recorded the event and wrote about it. Or 2. He did something amazing and your father heard stories about it passed down through the generations and then he wrote about it.

Emma: Obviously if my great, great, great, great grandfather's son recorded the event, it would contain a more precise account of what actually happened. By the time my father wrote about it, I could not necessarily trust the events that took place. By that time "legendary embellishment" would have occurred.

Sean: Excellent! Now, what if not only your great, great, great, great grandfather's son recorded the event, but also another son and two of his best friends? Would that help you to believe more in the historicity of the event?

Emma: Way more. Now I would believe we were onto something concrete.

Sean: Well, that's what we have with the New Testament! We have very early, multiple independent sources, writing about the life, death, and resurrection of Jesus. If there are several early independent sources recording the same event, we can trust it as reliable history. Historians believe that by just finding two independent sources it is like hitting the jackpot, but we have even more than that for the New Testament.

Emma: That is pretty cool. You are using history and some scientific techniques to show the credibility of Scripture. That is impressive. You are not just saying like others have that, "the Bible is the Word of God because the Bible says so."

Sean: That is circular reasoning. I do believe the Bible is the inspired Word of God, but I need to give a reason for it. Remember that historians depend on historical data from archaeology, ancient documents, and the testimony of eyewitnesses to uncover the past and separate what is fact from fiction. It is important to know that the Gospels are not written as fantasy and legend, but rather as historical narrative. These are not stories like "Johnny Appleseed," but rather the life and times of Jesus of Nazareth.

Listen to how Luke the Evangelist begins his account: "Since many have undertaken to compile a narrative of the events that have been fulfilled among us, just as those who were eyewitnesses from the beginning and ministers of the word have handed them down to us, I too have decided, after investigating everything accurately anew, to write it down in an orderly sequence for you, most excellent Theophilus, so that you may realize the certainty of the teachings you have received" (Luke 1:1-4).

This is not how legends are written. This is how a historian works.

Emma: I see that. He is insisting that we understand that he is really researching the truth of actual events.

Sean: C.S. Lewis, who wrote *The Lion, the Witch and the Wardrobe* and the other Narnia books, wrote this about the Gospels: "I have been reading poems, romances, vision-literature, legends, myths all my life. I know what they are like. I know that not one of them is like this." No one who takes the time to read the Gospels or epistles can come away thinking that they are old legend stories, and both historians and Scripture scholars agree with Lewis.

The Scriptures not only hold up to the historian's tests but prove to be head and shoulders above the rest of the ancient documents that have been discovered.

Emma: Can you give me an example? I would think that by the time we have received the Gospels, they would be greatly distorted because they were written down so many times through the years.

Sean: Yes, I can give you multiple examples, and no, the Scriptures have not been distorted. No other book of antiquity can even compare to that of the Bible for its historical reliability and accuracy! For example, *The Iliad*, written by Homer (not Simpson), was written in 700 B.C., and the earliest copy we have of it is 400 B.C. There is a 300-year gap between when it was written and the earliest copy we have of it, and only 643 copies have been discovered. Plato's writings were written in 400 B.C., and the earliest copy we have is A.D. 900. There is a 1,300-year gap between when it was written and the earliest copy we have—with only seven copies. The New Testament of the Bible was written around A.D. 40-90, and the earliest copies we have are from A.D. 114 (fragments) to A.D. 325 (complete New Testament). That makes only a 50-year gap between when it was written and the earliest fragments and copies we have of it. And there are more than 5,000 manuscripts! Nobody questions these other texts, so we should be even more confident in the Scriptures!

A.N. Sherwin-White, a professional historian who specializes in the times of Jesus and earlier, has written that the ancient manuscripts of Roman and Greek history are removed centuries from the original events they record. He gives an example of the two earliest biographies of Alexander the Great that were written by Arrian and Plutarch more than 400 years after Alexander's death, and yet classical historians still consider them to be trustworthy. The writings about Alexander that embellish his stories do not come until centuries after Arrian and Plutarch wrote their manuscripts. Sherwin-White believes it would take at least three generations to start wiping away the truth of the events recorded. When he speaks of the Gospels, he says that there is not enough time for the legends to arise because of the early writing of the Gospels.

This information gives more credibility to the New Testament as a historical document than any other ancient writing. You cannot accept the validity of these other ancient writings and still question the Gospels. The evidence clearly validates the Scriptures. See for yourself how the Bible measures up to other books of antiquity:

Title of Ancient Book	Date It Was Written	Date of Earliest Manuscript	Number of Manuscripts
Homer's *The Iliad*	700 B.C.	400 B.C.	643
Aristotle	384-322 B.C.	A.D. 1100	49
History of Herodotus	425 B.C.	A.D. 900	8
Caesar	100-44 B.C.	A.D. 900	10
Josephus' Jewish Wars	A.D. 70	A.D. 400	9
Histories of Tacitus	A.D. 100	A.D. 900	2
New Testament	A.D. 40-100	A.D. 114-145	5,366

So we can see that the New Testament Scriptures are the best-attested of all the books of antiquity. The Scriptures have more manuscripts and are written much more closely in time to the original events. This reveals that the New Testament we have today is almost exactly the same as the original copy! Only one percent of the words in the New Testament are in doubt, but those words in doubt are trivial and do nothing to change the meaning of any of the texts. Ninety-nine percent of the words in the New Testament are verified and accurate!

This is important to remember because it destroys the false claims that Muslims, Mormons, and others try to make on how the Scriptures were distorted. Those claims are verifiably incorrect. Think about this, Emma: When you read the words St. Paul penned in his jail cell in Rome, you are reading his exact words!

Emma: That is truly amazing. Why doesn't anyone ever tell us these things? Instead, we get these bogus programs on PBS about things like the Da Vinci Code.

Sean: I think we need to be accountable ourselves. People need to be good stewards of their time, and Jesus tells us, "Seek and you shall find," but how many people are actually seeking? I think people spend more time seeking entertainment than seeking God. I know I have to keep myself in check on that.

Emma: I can't argue that. I have used my anger and desire to live as I wanted to keep me from seeking truth and instead have only looked at resources that lined up with my faulty belief system.

Sean: Been there … done that. Now let's look at archeology. Time and time again, whenever historians have doubted the veracity of historical claims made by the Scriptures, archaeology comes through and shows that the Scriptures were right all along.

Emma: For example?

Sean: In 1961, a mosaic from the third century was found in Caesarea Maritima that had the name "Nazareth" in it. This is the first-known ancient non-biblical reference to Nazareth.

Coins with the names of the Herod family have been discovered, including the names of Herod the king, Herod the tetrarch of Galilee (who killed John the Baptist), Herod Agrippa I (who killed James Zebedee), and Herod Agrippa II (before whom Paul testified).

In 1990, an ossuary was found, inscribed with the Aramaic words, "Joseph son of Caiaphas," believed to be a reference to the high priest Caiaphas.

In 1968, an ossuary was discovered near Jerusalem bearing the bones of a man who had been executed by crucifixion in the first century. These are the only known remains of a man crucified in Roman Palestine, and they verify the descriptions given in the Gospels of Jesus' crucifixion.

In June 1961, Italian archaeologists excavating an ancient Roman amphitheater near Caesarea-on-the-Sea (Maritima) uncovered a limestone block. On its face is an inscription (part of a larger dedication to Tiberius Caesar) that reads: "Pontius Pilate, Prefect of Judaea."

Many other discoveries keep crushing the false notion that the Gospels are just legends and myths filled with fictional people and stories.

Emma: You are clobbering my ignorant ideas about the Bible. It's just that today we're bombarded with people saying so many erroneous things about the Bible.

Sean: I know. There is a lot of garbage that gets promoted out there about the Scriptures and the Church, but that's why we need to do our own work so we can cut through the smoke screen and find the truth.

Emma: How about a couple more questions, then? Are you saying that we have to believe everything in the Bible as true—such as God making the world in six days?

Sean: I think you already know the answer to that one, since I have been using the Big Bang as an evidence for God's existence. I get what you are trying to say, though. This is where people really get messed up when reading the Bible, and this is why God gave us the Church to help us from making these mess-ups that often lead many astray from the Christian faith.

The Scriptures themselves confirm that people without the guidance of the Church eventually get lost: "… our beloved brother Paul, according to the wisdom given to him, also wrote to you, speaking of these things as he does in all his letters. In them there are some things hard to understand that the ignorant and unstable distort to their own destruction, just as they do the other scriptures" (2 Peter 3:16). Even back when St. Paul was writing, people were twisting his words to fit with their own heretical beliefs!

That being said, let's go straight to the Church so she can explain the answer to you.

The Catechism of the Catholic Church states, "The reader must be attentive to what the human authors truly wanted to affirm and to what God wanted to reveal to us by their words" (CCC 109). Furthermore, "in order to discover the sacred authors' intention," the Catechism states, "the reader must take into account the conditions of their times and culture, the literal genres in use at that time, and the modes of feeling, speaking, and narrating then current" (CCC 110).

Emma: Can you explain that more to me?

Sean: Sure, the Church is saying that the Bible presents truth through many different ways of writing, such as: historical narrative, prophecy, poetry, etc.

The Scriptures are the inspired Word of God written though men. The Catechism states, "God inspired the human authors of the sacred books. To compose the sacred books, God chose certain men who, all the while he employed them in this task, made full use of their own faculties and powers so that, though he acted in them and by them, it was as true authors that they consigned to writing whatever he wanted written, and no more."

These men, while inspired by the Holy Spirit, wrote from different time periods and traditions and used different genres to do so.

Emma: So basically what the Church is saying is that we would be foolish to read the Bible as we would read a science book.

Sean: Exactly. If you read the creation accounts in Genesis as a science book, you are going to be very confused! It was not written as a science book. It is poetry revealing deep theological truths about the Author of creation and our rebellion against Him—and much, much more, but it is **not** written as a science text to prove that the universe is only 5,000 years old. It is okay to believe that if you want because it has no bearing on our salvation, but just so you know, the Church has not held as a doctrine that the universe is only 5,000 years old. In fact, many of the early Church fathers spoke in opposition to that. Could you imagine God trying to explain evolution, the Big Bang, and quarks to Moses?!

See if this helps: If you had a small child and wanted to teach her math, would you start with calculus or one apple plus two apples equals three apples?

Emma: The apples, of course.

Sean: God was giving Moses apples.

Emma: I get it.

Sean: Good ... but yet, I actually hate that analogy because it belittles how amazing the creation account truly is when interpreted correctly. It is so deep and rich.

Emma: It does help me to understand, though. But here's a question for you: Could these authors make errors?

Sean: Let's check with the Church in the Catechism again: "The inspired books teach the truth. Since therefore all that the inspired authors or sacred writers affirm should be regarded as affirmed by the Holy Spirit, we must acknowledge that the books of Scripture firmly, faithfully, and **without error** teach that truth which God, for the sake of our salvation, wished to see confided to the Sacred Scriptures."

Just as Jesus was fully God and fully man at the same time and could not sin, neither could the human authors inspired by the Holy Spirit write in error. While they used their own styles of writing, their inspiration comes from God. Once again, most people make the error of reading Scripture as you would a twenty-first-century textbook, and that is where so much trouble comes from.

The great Theologian and Doctor of the Church St. Thomas Aquinas wrote that the authors of Scripture wrote what God wanted, but in a way that men could understand and to which they were accustomed.

Think about it: If God is trying to reach the world, would He use only one genre? Would He only describe Himself in scientific ways?

Emma: No, I guess not.

Sean: Of course not! Science is a great tool, but it's not the only way we gain knowledge or understand things. For example, do you love your mother?

Emma: Yes I do, very much.

Sean: Scientifically explain that.

Emma: What? I can't.

Sean: Scientifically explain beauty.

Emma: Okay, I get your point.

Sean: Say there is no God, and one day you have a child. He or she asks you, "Mommy do you love me?" If there is no God, you will have to answer, "No, honey, love does not exist. What I am experiencing is a fluctuation of random neurons and electrons in my brain causing a sensation, and that sensation I have labeled as 'love.'"

Emma: Oh my …

Sean: God … is bigger than science. Science naturally flowed forth from the order of the universe that He created. He brought forth science, so He will not be pigeonholed by being defined by it. God IS love. Science helps us to understand how reasonable it is to have faith in God, but you don't use science to fall in love with someone. God doesn't want us to just believe in Him. The devil "believes" in Him. God wants us to fall in love with Him because He loved us first! Remember that even miracles did not win everyone over to God. God's holy Scriptures reach out to all humanity in a way that no other book can. Maybe it's the story of how Jesus heals the leper that touches your heart, or maybe it is the romance of Song of Songs that will captivate your heart—or Peter walking on the water.

The Bible is the story of God's walk with His people—how He slowly revealed Himself more intimately to them as their hearts became ready. He starts with a couple (Adam and Eve), then moves on to a family (Noah), then a tribe (Abraham), a nation (Moses), a kingdom (David), then … He comes Himself (Jesus) to sacrifice His life for the forgiveness of sins and to build us His Church so we can receive Him into our very bodies through the Eucharist.

Emma: Wow. So the Scriptures are able to reach the hearts of all because there is something in it for everyone and they are written in a universal way.

Sean: The Bible is not some antiquated book that was lost in translation as some so-called teachers would have you believe. The Scriptures are trustworthy when read within the protection of the Church because she is the final authority on how they are to be interpreted.

Emma: That makes sense or else we would have the "Build-a-Bear" problem with the Bible that we have with "spiritual" people who don't have the Church guiding them.

Sean: Correct. As I had mentioned, when people read the Bible without the protection of the Church, they twist the Scriptures to fit their lifestyle and make God in their own image.

Emma: After learning all of this, I have a whole new respect for the Bible.

Sean: I bet if you read and consume the words of Jesus, He will win your heart over. After all, love is what you have been looking for your whole life. Jesus is Love.

Chapter 10

Question 3: What Is the Meaning of Life?

Sean: So this leads us to the THIRD and FINAL question: What is the meaning of life? I touched on this earlier, but I want to really bring it home again.

Emma: Been dying for this answer!

Sean: We were made for this reason and this reason alone: to come to know and love God with all our heart, mind, soul, and strength. When we die, God will ask us, "Did you really love me? Did you keep my commandments? Did you confess your sins? Did you care for my lost and lonely and poor? Did you tell the world about Jesus? Did you use your gifts to bring glory to God?" The answers to those questions will determine our final destiny. Archbishop Fulton Sheen said, "When we die, we will hear the words, 'You're mine.' It will either be Jesus or Satan."

Emma: That would have made me be angry before, but now I understand. God can't force us to love Him, and He can't force us against our will to go to heaven. Hell is a choice of our own. God wants us all with Him.

Sean: Exactly. Think about it: God, who does not need us, created us and loves us so much He willingly died on a cross to redeem us, yet so many people don't really care. How often do you see people say grace in public

132

anymore? How many Christians have ever told another person about their faith in Christ? But that is exactly what we are commissioned by Jesus to do. In fact, a Christian is not really living fully until he does become a witness of Christ. It's like a beautiful Steinway that sits in the corner covered with dust—its beauty isn't perfected because it isn't making any music. The music of a Christian witnessing the faith in word and action is more beautiful to God and the angels and saints in heaven than any orchestra.

Remember, we are not selling a product. We are sharing the love of God, which is a love that is so powerful that it can heal all wounds and cure death. It is so sad that peer pressure and intolerance have made an impact on the faithful to the point where they think it's almost rude to share the love of Christ.

Emma: It's true. Today it feels like you can say the name of God but not the name of Jesus.

Sean: When you say the name "God," it's not that offensive because people make the name God mean anything their minds want. The name "God" is generic in today's world. But if you say the name "Jesus" … heads will turn. Jesus breaks all the rules. He upsets people. He makes people make a decision. Is He God or not? If He is, then we have to listen to Him. If He's not, then no big deal.

Emma: If He's not, then He's just a liar or a lunatic.

Sean: Correct. But if He's God, then He built a Church. Remember again Jesus' words: "And so I say to you, you are Peter, and upon this rock I will build my church, and the gates of the netherworld will not prevail against it" (Matthew 16:18). And He commands us to listen to it. Jesus said, "Whoever listens to you listens to me. Whoever rejects you rejects me. And whoever rejects me rejects the one who sent me" (Luke 10:16). And He commissioned us, "Go, therefore, and make disciples of all nations, baptizing them in the name of the Father and of the Son and of the Holy Spirit, teaching them to observe all that I have commanded you. And behold, I am with you always, until the end of the age" (Matthew

28:19-20). While Jesus was addressing the Church here, showing that He would protect it and guide it, the Church has clearly charged us with the same mission of making disciples of Christ.

Remember, it is dangerous business making a God who will bow to your every whim. The man who says, "God told me it's okay to leave my wife and children because He wants me to be happy," and the woman who says, "God told me it's okay to abort my child," are perfect examples of the self-made God who is more like a slave to its owner's condition. God would never say those things. He already spoke on these issues, and He would never contradict Himself.

Emma: I have such a different picture in my mind now about Jesus. I always thought of Him as Gentle Jesus, meek and mild, almost like a frail philosopher.

Sean: Yeah, I have heard people say that before, and they couldn't be further from the truth. I dare not put Jesus in a box because He is God, but when we read the Scriptures we find a warrior unlike any warrior in history. He fought with love and humility. He fought for us, to save us … but we reject Him so often. He IS love, and one day we will give an account of our lives before Him.

Emma: Sounds scary.

Sean: For those who lived for the world and did not truly love and serve the Lord, it will be. Think about it: God created us out of love, and we betray Him. He offers His only begotten Son (Jesus, the second Person of the Trinity) to die on a cross for the forgiveness of our sins and build us a Church—and we still sin. And all we have to do is go to confession to receive His infinite forgiveness—and we still don't go. He gives us His Body at Mass to strengthen us with His love to lead us to holiness—and people don't go.

Emma: We are so ungrateful!

Sean: We all are from time to time, but many never give thanks. They seem to have forgotten that one day they will die and stand before the Just Judge, Jesus, who will hold out His hands with holes in them from the nails of His crucifixion, and give an account for their lives. There are also those who haven't forgotten that they will die, but they rely on the "God" they made up in their own minds to be there with arms wide open, telling them what amazing people they are even though they did not help the poor, confess their sins, or attend Mass except on Easter and Christmas.

Emma: Are you afraid of Judgment Day?

Sean: Yes, I am.

Emma: Why? You love God!

Sean: I do love God, but I still sin. I'm afraid because, while Jesus forgives my sins when I confess, I still have to look into His eyes and know that after all He has done for me, I still sinned. I can't imagine the hurt I cause Him. Sin is a betrayal of my friendship and love of Him. The good news is that I hate when I sin and I confess my sins. God is merciful, and He knows that I'm trying to grow in holiness. I trust that God will perfect me when I am in His presence and wipe away every tear and make all things new.

Emma: So you are confident you are going to heaven?

Sean: I am not confident in myself at all; I know how weak I am. I put my trust and confidence in our amazing God, who is full of mercy and forgiveness. I dare not judge myself a saint and declare that I am going to heaven. I am working out my salvation with fear and trembling, as St. Paul says in Philippians 2:12. Now this isn't to make us paranoid freaks, but rather to encourage us to finish the race well. Growing in holiness is a lifelong process, and while I am far from it now, I pray one day to be a saint. When I meet Jesus, I want to meet Him bloodied and battered from proclaiming His love to the world. He died for me, and I pray I will die to myself for Him.

Emma: Being a follower of Jesus is completely different than what I thought it would be. I have had some Christians really hurt me before and tell me I'm going to hell. It really turned me off from Jesus.

Sean: I'm so sorry to hear that, Emma. While there are times for correction among brothers and sisters in Christ, it should be done with love and charity. We are supposed to encourage and guide each other along. Always remember this, though: Never judge a religion by its followers, but rather by its founder.

There are hypocrites in every religion and philosophy. Don't leave Jesus because of the sins of others. Learn to forgive and pray for your enemies as our Lord commands us. There is great freedom when you can forgive your enemies. They no longer have any power over you. Give control of your life to God and not to people who insult you.

One more thing. Being a Christian doesn't mean we are better than anyone else. It just means that we recognize what train wrecks we are and how much we need Jesus to save us.

Emma: Got it.

Sean: Emma, I could go on forever about this amazing faith God has given us, but I think I will let you do some work on your own now. That's how I will know that it really made an impact on you. But before I give you homework, do you have the answers to the three most important questions a person can ask?

Emma: Yes, I do. 1. God exists. The evidence is pretty overwhelming from a scientific point of view and philosophical one, as well. 2. Jesus is God. God is personal and not some distant obscure blob in space. He is also not something I create in my own mind but, rather, *He* created *me*. 3. He created me to know and love Him and spread His word to the world.

Sean: Amen, Emma. You listened. Now it's time for some homework. I'm going to give you some websites and books to read. Some are more difficult than others, but all are worth reading. I don't get paid to promote any of these works. These are just the ones that helped me find my way among hundreds of others. I think these are the foundational books and works to get you started.

After you digest this information, I can't wait to speak with you again and have you teach *me*! You will get so excited as you continue to see that this faith is not only of the heart, but can also be investigated through reason. There are actual answers to the important questions—and they lead to the Truth. I can make a promise to you: When you truly see that all of this is not just a fairy tale, but a beautiful reality, your life will never be the same.

Resources for Life

1. The Catholic Answers website (www.catholic.com) contains the answers to most of your questions regarding the faith. Just type in the search bar, and you'll be amazed at the resources. Every Catholic needs to know about this website!

2. *www.reasonablefaith.org*. William Lane Craig is, in my opinion, the best defender of the faith on the topic of the existence of God and the resurrection of Jesus. He can be really lofty at times, but he has materials for every level. Please get his book, *On Guard, Defending Your Faith with Reason and Precision*. This is one of the best books I have read for laypeople starting out to learn about the existence of God and the resurrection. You can also watch any of his debates on YouTube.

3. Trent Horn's book, *Answering Atheism*, is fantastic. Read it!

4. N.T. Wright is one of my heroes. You will find no work on the resurrection superior to his book, *The Resurrecton of the Son of God*. He demolishes all other theories and demonstrates why the resurrection is the best explanation for the rise of the Christian faith. This book, however, is almost 800 pages long. I have read it twice because I have had the time. You can get great information from the book by reading his essays. Google, "N.T. Wright and crucifixion and evidence and mutations."

5. Scott Hahn's book, *Rome Sweet Home*, is a must. It's about his conversion from Protestantism to Catholicism.

6. *Born Fundamentalist, Born Again Catholic* by David Currie is also a must.

7. Read Peter Kreeft's books, *A Refutation of Moral Relativism: Interviews with an Absolutist* and *How to Win the Culture War: A Christian Battle Plan for a Society in Crisis.*

Also, you can read or listen to Kreeft's work *How to Lose the Culture war.* Check it out on YouTube: https://www.youtube.com/watch?v=tm08x8YiuXk#t=40

8. When you want to be a total master, read these by G.K. Chesterton: *The Everlasting Man* and *Orthodoxy.*

9. If you like newspapers and great websites for news, then I highly recommend the *National Catholic Register* and their website *ncregister.com.* Best Catholic newspaper on the market.

Author's Note

Please know that the sales of this book go to help fund our mission serving the poorest of the poor in Haiti: Haiti180. Find it online at haiti180.com. The sale of any of my music—at seanforrest.com—also goes to help our mission. Thank you!